George W Isham

Two Years in India

Or, Some Missionary Lessons, and how They Were Learned

George W Isham

Two Years in India
Or, Some Missionary Lessons, and how They Were Learned

ISBN/EAN: 9783337060251

Printed in Europe, USA, Canada, Australia, Japan

Cover: Foto ©ninafisch / pixelio.de

More available books at **www.hansebooks.com**

TWO YEARS IN INDIA;

OR,

SOME MISSIONARY LESSONS, AND HOW THEY WERE LEARNED.

BY

REV. GEO. W. ISHAM,
OF THE NEBRASKA CONFERENCE.

CINCINNATI:
PRINTED FOR THE AUTHOR BY CRANSTON & CURTS,
1893.

GOD'S MESSAGE TO THE CHURCH.

"Enlarge the place of thy tent, and let them stretch forth the curtains of thine habitations: spare not, lengthen thy cords, and strengthen thy stakes; for thou shalt break forth on the right hand and on the left; and thy seed shall inherit the Gentiles, and make the desolate cities to be inhabited."

—Isa. LIV, 2, 3.

Copyright
By Geo. W. Isham.
1893.

PREFACE.

THE greatest need of the Church, aside from its constant spiritual awakening from on high, is information from the fields beyond. If it were possible to let the disciples of Jesus in Christian lands see the need of their brethren in heathenism, and to know the power of the gospel to deliver them from the strongholds of evil, in whose bonds they are helpless, missionary going and giving would be increased many fold.

The information needed is many-sided, requiring fullness of detail; and it seems that missionaries and their home authorities have been so absorbed in the work at the front, that they have been unable to so inform the great body of Church members as to keep them sympathetically enlisted with them. It has often seemed to the writer that if the people at home were better acquainted with the missionaries they are supporting, and knew more of their experiences and toils, they would more vividly realize that the present missionary movement is not an enterprise undertaken by a mere handful of enthusiasts, which they are called to help, more for charity's sake than for any other reason; but would see that it is a forward movement of the whole Church, widening the circumference of evangelism; and that the missionaries are our sent agents, who can win us victories only as we furnish them the sinews of war. It is the purpose of this little book to take the reader through two years of missionary experience, and let him learn some of the lessons those two years taught, in the hope that practical missionary devotion, expressed in earnest prayer and sacrifice to give, may be, to some extent, increased.

G. W. I.

FAIRBURY, NEBRASKA, January, 25, 1893.

CONTENTS.

PART I.—EXPERIENCE.

CHAPTER I.
THE CALL AND PREPARATION, ... 7

CHAPTER II.
THE TRIP. 13

CHAPTER III.
FIRST IMPRESSIONS, ... 40

CHAPTER IV.
AT WORK, ... 58

CHAPTER V.
A LETTER FROM THE FIELD, ... 65

CHAPTER VI.
AN IMPORTANT EVENT, ... 75

CHAPTER VII.
MOVING FORWARD, ... 84

CHAPTER VIII.
THE SECOND YEAR, ... 90

CHAPTER IX.
THE ENGLISH WORK, ... 101

CHAPTER X.
DIVERSIONS, ... 108

CHAPTER XI.
Conquered by Broken Health, ... 118

CHAPTER XII.
Homeward Travels, ... 133

PART II.—MISSIONARY LESSONS.

CHAPTER I.
The Work and its Magnitude, ... 148

CHAPTER II.
Perversions of Paganism, ... 156

CHAPTER III.
Perversion of Religious Ideas, ... 167

CHAPTER IV.
Women in Paganism, ... 173

CHAPTER V.
The Conservatism of Paganism, ... 179

CHAPTER VI.
Benefits of the British Empire, ... 185

CHAPTER VII.
Hindrances from Christian Lands, ... 191

CHAPTER VIII.
The Gospel the Only Hope, ... 200

CHAPTER IX.
Responsibility of Stewardship, ... 210

Two Years in India.

PART I.—EXPERIENCE.

Chapter I.

THE CALL AND PREPARATION TO GO.

AT the session of the Nebraska Annual Conference held in St. Paul's Church, Lincoln, in the fall of 1887, Bishop J. M. Thoburn—then Dr. Thoburn—was present on Sunday, and spoke at night on India and his eventful experience as a missionary there. I suppose I was not differently nor more deeply affected by what he said than were others. No one can hear Bishop Thoburn speak without being impressed with the simple grace and directness of his style, his entire freedom from conceits and affectation of every sort; and his masterly grasp and marshaling of the leading facts of the missionary situation must furnish any true Christian who hears him the basis of a permanent missionary inspiration. But we were so situated at the time that we could go at once. And when the speaker, in closing, said, "Perhaps the call to go comes to some of you young men here to-night. If it does not, do not think of going; but if it does come, go; and God will be with you," I felt strangely moved. And when I came to myself, I found that I was fighting my own convictions by saying over and over to myself: "It does not come to me. It does not come to me."

I had just before this Conference been through an unusual season of religious refreshing, and had learned the beginning of what it means to be entirely consecrated to God, and to definitely receive the Holy Spirit as an indwelling Master, and to be led by him in all things, only, however, according to the spirit and the letter of God's Word. So that, when I found myself inwardly resisting the sense of duty, I was convinced I was resisting the Spirit's call, and at once surrendered to go—this provided, of course, that my wife was of the same mind; for I do not believe that God calls the husband and not the wife, nor *vice versa*. He might call them to a work that would require them to separate in order to accomplish it; but if they were both in communion with him, they would both be convinced of his will, and reconciled to do it. They would both see that it was the highest duty, and would make whatever of sacrifice it involved, gladly, for Jesus sake!

I went home to York, Nebraska, on Monday after the Conference; and, after chatting awhile, I told my wife some of the things that Bishop Thoburn had said in his address, and of the needed missionaries for India. I said nothing to her of my own convictions; and, to my surprise, she came to me an hour or two after, and proposed that we offer ourselves to go. We settled to do so, and sent our application at once to the Missionary Board. While we were awaiting our acceptance, we went to Weeping Water, Nebraska, our appointment, and began work.

I had been teaching in the York College the year previous; but during the summer we had decided to permanently retire from educational work, and enter directly the work of the ministry, as God and the Church should direct. So, excepting our household effects, we were all sold out and ready to go anywhere. After Conference, we were so certain we were going to India, simply because God was leading that way, that we sold our furniture and everything we could not take with us, at once, and before we were formally accepted by the Board.

It was about five weeks after Conference before we received the word which made us foreign missionaries. These five weeks were full of temptation and trial to us. Our relatives used every influence of ridicule, argument, and affectionate persuasion to overcome our convictions. And some well-meaning friends were sure we were forfeiting the most flattering prospects of usefulness and honor in the Church by our, to them, "inexplicable move." But none of these influences changed the fact of our conviction that God called us to go. Again and again my good wife said: "I feel that there is but one thing for us to do. I feel that we could not succeed in any work in this country. We must go." For my own part, I felt that to yield to the persuasions of loved ones against our convictions—which were according to God's Word, and were always strengthened by communion with God in prayer—was to give to human relationships a higher authority than to the Divine; was to obey man rather than God. Still there were some who encouraged us to do what we felt was God's will, and some urged us to go. These friends helped us greatly. And so the days went by; and at last a letter came from Dr. J. M. Reid—then corresponding secretary of the Missionary Society—stating that we were appointed, and that our passage had been arranged for by the Anchor Line Steamship Company, to sail in twelve days.

Mrs. Isham went at once to visit with loved ones in Indiana, while I got our affairs in order, packed our boxes, and closed up our work in

Weeping Water. I expressed our goods to New York, because the time was too short for them to go by freight, and hurried on to join my family *en route*. An insignificant affair occurred the morning we left the old home at Liberty, Indiana, for New York, which shows so clearly that the leadership of the Holy Spirit does not save one from mistakes nor render it unnecessary that he should have his wits about him and use his God-given common sense, that I take the space to tell it. We started from Liberty on our long journey nearly half-way round the world. We were in all haste to get to New York. We changed cars at Hamilton, Ohio. The road by which we were to go branches just after leaving Hamilton, one branch going to Chicago, and the other toward New York. The trains came in near together. The Chicago train came first. Though it was not quite time yet for our train, I got us all aboard it without a question. The conductor did not come through till we were well out of Hamilton, and our train would be gone before we could get back. We had a wait of four hours at a station called Seven Mile, and were delayed twenty-four hours. The Spirit leads us in the high realms of conviction and spiritual enlightenment; but an ordinary man has sense enough, if he will only use it, to inquire the destination of a train before he boards it. Fortunately, however, our ship did not sail as soon as we expected, and we had nearly two days with friends in the city. Saturday evening we boarded the Anchor Line steamship *Devonia*; and, amid the noise and disorder of lading and final preparation, we endured and enjoyed what Bishop Thoburn told us was the beginning of missionary life. The bishop suggested that our experience would begin in earnest when we came to the luxury of seasickness.

Chapter II.

THE TRIP.

A LANDLUBBER often has many dreamy notions of the delight and luxury connected with a steamship passage across the Atlantic. But there was nothing of the kind in our November voyage. We sailed to Glasgow, and were told nine days would see us anchored in the Clyde; but our ship did not reach the Glasgow docks till the morning of the thirteenth day. The storms provided entertainment from which our good ship could not withdraw for four days. Perhaps a brief description of the trip in general will be interesting.

All the Saturday night after we went aboard the most terrific noise was kept up by the lading machinery, the thumping of boxes, the shouting of the dock men, and the hurried tramping overhead. In spite of it all, however, we were soundly sleeping, when, at about three o'clock in the morning, the steward awakened us with the shout: "We are about to sail!" We went on deck; saw them remove the gangplanks, unfasten the hawsers, and, amid the noise of hurrying preparation and the hoarse shouts of the sailors calling their commands from one to another, the steam was turned on; a concert of roar and hiss and sizzle came from below, and our ship began to move and tremble and creak like a great sphere about to burst by the pressure of its own inward forces.

As we moved farther out, toward the open sea, the scene became to me very impressive: with the splendid array of lights along the shore behind us; the far-stretching sea of darkness before us, illumined by a single yet resplendent light—that held aloft by the Statue of Liberty on Bedloe's Island. The scene was so suggestive of the life we imagined we were entering upon: all the multitude of lights of the beautiful life and civilization of America left behind us, the darkness of heathenism before, and Jesus—the only Star of Liberty—to enlighten the gloom! When I sail out of New York harbor again, I shall have more sense than to imagine such unreal likenesses. For the fact is, when one sets out to be a missionary, he at once puts himself in direct touch with the highest and best enlightenment, culture, and civilization on the face of the earth. He goes, taking his civilization with him, and his companions and associates are the leaders in the world's civilization. There are also far more of the facilities and conveniences of Western civilization in India than Americans, as a rule, imagine.

From such meditations, however, we were awakened by the shouts of the sailors, who were rigging the sails, crying, "Heave-ho! heave!" for well we knew that we passengers would be giving unwilling obedience, shortly, in a manner unthought of by them. Sunday was a beautiful day. The sea was quiet, and none of our party were sick. By Monday noon we had gone three hundred and fourteen miles. This day was also fair; but the wind was pretty strong, the sea roughened in the afternoon, Neptune levied tribute on me, and I showed what I had in me. Tuesday morning was fair, and the sea smooth, and we all felt well. We made two hundred and eighty-eight miles from noon Monday to noon Tuesday. In the afternoon the weather became heavy. A terrific gale of a head-wind set in; the anger of the sea increased, till our old ship rolled and plunged beyond all description. The ship did not unlade, but the passengers tried to give up even more than they had. I think we would have cast our immortal souls into the sea, had it been possible. In penance and anguish that we had ever eaten anything, we refused to be nourished or dressed on Wednesday; but spent the long, tempestuous hours trying to let ourselves down easily, first on one and then on the other side of the berth, as the waves tossed our ship about.

As soon as the sea became rough, a collection-pan was fastened to the side of each berth, about a foot below the pillow. A most unkind arrangement, for the thing acts like a stomach-pump! Wednesday was a very hard day, and we made but two hundred and forty-six miles. Thursday morning was a little better, and some of our party began to crawl out to see what was left of us; but no member of our family could go to the table. We toned up on Liebig's chicken-broth and beef-extract. Thursday's log was two hundred and thirty-eight miles. Friday morning every one was better, and out on deck. The weather was favorable, with a strong north wind. We made three hundred miles—schedule speed for the *Devonia*. Saturday repeated Friday's experience and speed. Saturday night the weather became heavy again; still, we made three hundred miles to Sunday noon. I was to have preached on Sunday morning, but seasickness set in again with the rough weather; and my second attack lasted three days, and was much severer than the first. The ship had a hard trial in this storm. We made but two hundred and thirty-five miles from Sunday to Monday noon, and but one hundred and eighty-one miles from Monday to Tuesday noon. The sailors called it a "stiff gale," and the captain's face wore an expression of extreme anxiety. Monday night the storm was so fierce that the engines were shut down, and the ship given over to the mercy of the wind and waves. The ship rolled and pitched till one had all he could do to stay in his berth. The seamen unfurled a sail, thinking thereby to steady the ship somewhat; but when the wind got hold of it, it tore it to strings. One can imagine something of the force of the wind when he remembers that these sails are made of the very strongest canvas. The waves ran so high and with such force as to stave in a lifeboat suspended above the hurricane-deck. The wind blew sixty or seventy miles an hour. The sea presented a scene so terrifically grand that no one short of genius would attempt to describe it. The waves seemed like mountains chasing one another. It seemed that square miles of the sea were being lifted to the skies in a body; and everywhere on the surface the waves ran together, and crests were bursting, producing the wildest scene of flying spray and dancing foam.

There was one, to me, supreme moment in this storm. It was about midnight, Monday. The machinery—except the pumps—was still.

The wind and the waves handled our ship as though it were a bubble. The heavy waves thundered on the deck above, the hungry yawn of the sea could be distinctly heard, now and then the shrill scream of the seagull sounded like a note of despair, we had eaten considerably less than nothing for three days, and the dull thumping of the pumps below suggested a sinking ship. The darkness was intense. In the midst of such surroundings, I came from a sick sleep to semi-consciousness, and for a moment I was seized with indescribable terror. Just then, above the weird din of the tempest, rang out the strong, clear voice of the faithful watchman: "All's well!" This entirely awakened me; and, taking it as a word both of the watchman and the Faithful Father—by whose leading we were there—the sweet peace of a steady trust filled my mind, and I prayed: "O Father, in the midst of every storm of life, may I hear, above all else, thy Spirit's word, 'All's well! all's well!'"

Wednesday the weather became respectable again. We made our first landing that night at Moville, Ireland. Thursday morning we were skirting the north coast of Ireland. About us were islands in every direction. The scenery about the approaches to the Clyde is exceedingly picturesque. Unfortunately for us, November is a foggy month in those parts, and our view was not at all satisfactory.

We reached Greenock, at the mouth of the Clyde, in the afternoon; and, as our ship could not ascend to Glasgow till the tide rose, we went ashore on a tug, and went up by rail. We were much disappointed not to be able to ascend the river in daylight, for the scenery is said to be superb. Our landing was not at all an enjoyable affair. Very strict precautions were being taken at the time to prevent the landing of dynamiters and infernal machines. The inspection of our baggage was very minute, and we were detained on deck, exposed to the raw Scotch wind and a drizzling rain. The whole family contracted heavy colds. One rarely takes cold at sea, but it is difficult to land in cold weather without doing so.

We reached Glasgow about seven o'clock; and were glad indeed to be once more on solid ground, and to sit down before a grate-fire, in our neat and cozy room in the Hotel Cockburn (Coburn). The entire missionary party dined together at 8 P. M., and I am sure I never relished food more in my life than then. The food was no better, nor was it better prepared, nor was the service more costly, nor the attendance more elaborate and polite, than we would find in any good hotel in America; but a convalescent from six days' of violent seasickness has, on landing, an appetite so supremely potent that differences in character and flavor of food are of slight consequence to him. In one of my classes as a teacher, once, a tall, hungry-looking boy defined appetite as "an eternal desire for food" (the text-book said "internal"). And it seemed to me the boy was not far wrong in our particular case at that time. It was so with each member of the party. I remember to have frequently gone out, right after dinner or some other meal, to the baker's and fruit-stands, and come in loaded with sacks of buns, apples, and such things, to tide us over to the next meal.

Our missionary party across the Atlantic numbered fifteen, including the children: B. F. West, M. D., of Iowa, wife, and two children, bound for Singapore. Dr. West is still in the field, a successful missionary in Malaysia. Rev. E. F. Frease, of Ohio, wife, and baby girl. Brother Frease went out as pastor of the Fort Methodist Episcopal Church in Bombay, but has since become a successful missionary to the Gujarati people at Baroda, north of Bombay, where he is now stationed. Rev. A. E. Winter and wife, of Ohio, went subject to appointment on arrival. They were sent to Bellary, a station in the Deccan. Mr. Winter's health was not good long after arriving in India; and a little over a year later, his heroic wife was seized by a violent attack of black measles, and died in two days. Mr. Winter, shattered in health and overwhelmed with grief, returned to America. Miss Anna Thompson, of Ohio, a sister of Mrs. Frease, went out, not under appointment, but to enter the work, and has since become a regular Woman's Foreign Missionary Society missionary, working in Bombay. Miss Ada Proctor, of Illinois, went to India to become the wife of the Rev. Dr. Butcher, our missionary then at Moradabad. The morning after our arrival in Bombay we had the pleasure of attending the wedding. Dr. and Mrs. Butcher are still in the field. Miss M. E. Files, of New York, went out under the Woman's Foreign Missionary Society. She labored faithfully four years in Rangoon, Burmah, and came home in shattered health. Besides these, the writer, his wife, and baby girl, completed the number.

I was impressed with one thing in associating with these yokefellows, and that is, that missionaries are not materially different from common Christian humanity. They are just as likely to have narrow prejudices and foibles of weakness as other Christians; and, as I learned afterward, are just as likely to make spiritual shipwreck in the storms of temptation which assail them. There is no calling nor life on earth where we do not have to "watch and pray," and work out our salvation with fear and trembling. But taken as a whole, the party has so far proven an exceptionally good one. None have brought disgrace upon the cause in any way; but one died; and but three so lost their health as to be compelled to return home, and these, it is likely, will all return again to the work. Having described the party, I now return to the trip.

Off Greenock, in the harbor, we saw the *Great Eastern* at anchor. She no longer goes to sea; and the only revenue derived from her comes from running summer excursions down the Clyde, and charging a shilling to look her over. There, too, we saw *Ajax*, the largest British man-of-war, plated with ten-inch steel, and seemingly able to go through almost anything without harm.

We were surprised at the politeness of the porters, baggage-carriers, and cab-drivers everywhere. On landing, one of them came near, bowed, stood at a respectful distance, and offered his services. As we needed him to carry luggage and show us the way, I engaged him. He carried our two heavy satchels a quarter of a mile, showed us to an apartment in the car, politely answered all our questions; and when I asked him his bill, he said, "What you please, sir." I paid him a shilling (24 cents), and he seemed much pleased. Americans, when they first land, pay more than these servants would charge; so it pays them to trust to our generosity. But when one learns that he is expected to tip everybody that in any way helps on his existence and plans, he becomes necessarily more conservative. These porters and railway attendants will go to any amount of trouble for you, never complain or speak short, treat one just as well when he rides third class as when he goes first class, and thankfully receive any little offer he is pleased to make them.

In picturing the appearance of the towns and cities of the Old World, one will be helped by remembering that they were built before the days of fourteen-story buildings and modern improvements. Hence, the buildings are seldom over three stories high; and, in most hotels, the water in your room is carried there by hand, and your light is a tallow candle—this, too, in the best hotels even in London.

The scene that greeted us when we looked from our hotel window over the tops of the houses was amusing at first sight; the chimney-stacks are so numerous! There are often eight or ten abreast on the edge of a flat roof, not over six inches or a foot apart, thirty or forty on a single housetop. They are from two to three feet high, and one can hardly imagine what a wilderness of them the housetops of a city present. Stone and yellow or brown brick are the only building materials used. The streets are stone, the sidewalks stone, the houses stone — stone everywhere, everything stone. Glasgow is a drab city—smoky and drab, aged, hoary, buried in gloom and haze and fog. But inside the houses and shops, everything is hale and cheery. The Scotch are hearty-looking, ruddy-faced, and sparkling-eyed. The children play in Glasgow—shout and run and laugh— have rosy cheeks, and look like rogues of fun and mischief. Even the ragged children play and seem happy.

We were in Glasgow two days, when, finding we had a week yet before we could sail from Liverpool, we started for London. We made the trip in daylight, Saturday, right through the heart of England. It was a delightful ride. I was surprised that we did not stop so often as trains do in America. The villages are not more than two or three miles apart; but the through trains stop only every twenty-five miles, on an average. The villages, as a rule, are small, often consisting of a single row of houses built together, and precisely alike. The station-houses are very fine, being built of red granite, and having wide and commodious platforms under cover. They are modern-looking, and quite ornamental. I did not see a frame building, of any kind, anywhere in Great Britain.

There is much more country, and less village and town, in England than one is likely to think. There are no spreading, mile-square villages of one hundred people, as are so often seen in America. A village of a hundred people occupies about as much space as an American farmer usually allots to his home and barn premises. Some of these villages look like barn, rather than home, premises. But usually they are tidy and homelike. The scenery everywhere is restful and inviting. The country is quite broken, and every nook and corner is cultivated like a garden. Fields, strewn with turnips as large as Dutch cheeses; flocks of sheep, feeding in green meadows; men, plowing with four large horses, tandem; a village here and there; an occasional ivy-mantled tower; an old-fashioned windmill; palatial country residences; here a timid glen, with the thread of a waterfall playing at hide-and-seek among the rocks and moss; and huge oaks and elms,

"That wreathe their old fantastic roots so high,"—

make up the picture of an English landscape.

The day passed quickly and delightfully, and at half-past seven in the evening we were in a room ten feet square, in the Arundel Hotel, in the heart of the greatest city in the world. Sabbath was our first day in London, and I went to St. Paul's Cathedral, the largest and most magnificent edifice of all Protestantism. I guessed the dome to be two hundred feet in circumference on the interior. At intervals there are panels on the inside of the dome to receive paintings of sacred scenes and persons. But they are, for the most part, blank. Portraits of Peter, Matthew, and of one or two other of the disciples, adorn the only panels yet in use. There are also many niches for busts and statues which are unoccupied. One is surrounded, though, by superb statues of England's greatest Churchmen, warriors, and statesmen. The marble steps leading to the main entrance are the length of half a square in an American town. The service was long, formal, and flat; and the giant stone pillars, vast arches, and stretching wastes of stone floor chill one in winter time. I was glad to find myself again at the hotel, greeted by the promising odor of the coming luncheon.

In the afternoon we went to Westminster Abbey. We were compelled to take our baby,

Anna, with us. She attracted so much attention—not because she was noisy, but because she was a babe in the Abbey—that we did not stay to the service. The English never take children of such tender years to church, and nothing seems more out of place to them. In the evening the gentlemen of the party attended services in a Wesleyan chapel on Queen's Street. The sermon was on the Prodigal Son. It was not eloquent, nor striking; but it *was* long. There was a large attendance, and evidently great earnestness among the worshipers. On one side, seated together, were as many as one hundred boys, averaging thirteen years of age, I judged. They were under the care of a gentleman, who sat in their midst. They were the best behaved company of boys of that age I have ever seen. A work of this sort could be done, by the right persons, in most Churches of two hundred or more members in America, with the best results both to the boys and to the Churches. One reason our boys do not go to Church is because they are not taught and organized to go. At the close of the sermon a very good prayer-meeting was held. The preacher started it, and then turned it over to a local preacher or exhorter. The meeting's purpose was to lead souls to accept Christ, and it was not unlike Methodist after-meetings in America. It was very enthusiastic, being participated in chiefly by young men.

When we reached the hotel we found our wives famishing, which reminded us that we, too, were unable to go till morning without food. We went out in a body to get oysters. We found a place on the great street called "The Strand." When one of us ordered eight milk-stews, the man said: "Height w'at?" We found that milk-stews, like many other dishes, are peculiar to America. We explained our desires, and the oysters were finally served. But they were very small—not larger than small hickory-nuts. We began to realize that the days of Baltimore "selects" were over with us for awhile. They cost, too, more than good oysters do in the Mississippi Valley, and we had to pay extra for the crackers, etc.

On Monday we found a private boarding-place, where we had more room and better accommodations every way than in the hotel. We got moved and settled, and in communication with the steamship company's office, and were free to use the balance of our delay sight-seeing.

Tuesday we visited the British Museum, and lost ourselves for the day in that world of antiquities and curiosities. It contains the history of the world on many lines: Of its art—in paintings and sculpture; of its literature—in ancient inscriptions, rolls, and manuscripts; of its governments—in signets, coins, and seals; of its religions—in images, mummies, and sacred writings; of its decay—in tombs, coffins, and the general dilapidation of all that remains of some of earth's greatest names and nations. The seal of King Darius, which sealed Daniel in the lion's den; the mummy of Cleopatra; the original parchment of *Magna Charta;* the contract for the sale of "Paradise Lost;" the Will of Mary Queen of Scots; Wycliffe's translation of the Bible; Cædmon's paraphrase; Hebrew Scriptures, on rolls of goat-skin; the Arabic Koran of Mohammed, also on goat skins; and an endless multitude of similar and dissimilar objects, interest and bewilder and weary one before he is half through.

Wednesday we visited the "Zoo"—as they say in London, when they mean the Zoological Gardens—which contains by far the largest and finest collection of animals in the world. It takes a whole day to wander through its many buildings, and one is wearied with the constant change and surprise.

Thursday we "did" Westminster Abbey. The beadle, who was our guide, pointed out to us the resting-places of a multitude of royal personages. He practiced the usual English boycott and dislocation of the letter *h;* and the solemn grandeur of the ancient pile, and the sacred ashes of departed royalty, were not sufficient to prevent our amusement from becoming audible, when our venerable guide struck the floor with his cane, and declaimed, in stentorian tones: "Hunder this hancient halabaster slab rest the hashes of the hinfant Hedward!" Besides the deceased of the royal family, there rest here the remains of noble persons without number, of a few literary lights, and of not a few great warriors and statesmen. There are not nearly so many tombs and memorials of literary persons as I had supposed. The bust of our own poet Longfellow is given a prominent place by his English admirers; but aside from him, no American is represented. The Abbey is somber and stately, and one of meditative mind would want to linger long among its aisles and chapels and ancient tombs; but a practical American regards it as a stately graveyard, and is glad to return to the busy life of the great city.

We wore ourselves out, Friday, visiting London Tower and South Kensington Museum. One must write a book to describe the Tower, and volumes to catalogue the Museum. The former was once the home of the English court.

It was built by William the Conqueror, but was much enlarged and elaborated after his time. The inclosure is quadrangular, surrounded by massive walls, which are surmounted by towers. To enter, one passes through the iron gateway of one of the towers of this outer wall, across the deep and now dry moat, and from thence into the outer circle of buildings, which are towers to the inner wall. There are a number of these buildings facing the central inclosure. They are solid, massive, and gloomy, and were used for States-prisons and as residences for the courtiers who were nearest the royal person. The prison-towers are dreadful. One involuntarily shudders as the creaking iron doors close behind him, and he remembers that the very steps of deep-worn stone that he is ascending have borne the trembling feet of martyrs and the innocent victims of royal crime, as well as the firm step of confident persecutors, and the cringing weight of assassins like Richard of Gloucester. In these gloomy cells the sighs and tears and prayers of saintly heroes have been known to God alone. In this circular apartment hundreds have been racked and pinched and tortured in a thousand nameless ways, and all for no other offense than fidelity to the truth which the world can not receive. And here is the cell of the doomed. One is forced to crawl to get into it. It is little more than large enough to turn around in, and as dark as Egyptian midnight. Latimer and Ridley were crowded in here, and a long list of others have found this the dark vestibule to eternity. On the walls of the common cells are many inscriptions, cut there by the prisoners of different centuries. The oldest is dated 1345. They are mostly in Latin, and are illustrated by the carving of the dove, and other Christian symbols. One inscription, translated, reads: "They who suffer most for Christ's sake in this life, glory most with him in the life to come." Within this inner wall of buildings are spacious grounds, which were once the king's gardens and walks. They are now used as parade and drill grounds for the soldiers. In the center stands the White Hall Palace, the ancient royal home. It is now used as an armory and jewel-house, where the crown-jewels are kept. This jewel-house is the room occupied by Henry VI during his long captivity through the reign of Edward IV. Under a great glass cover, at least ten feet in diameter, and surrounded by a strong and high iron fencing, the crowns of the different sovereigns from away back are kept. They are built up into a pyramid, surmounted by Victoria's crown, the largest and richest of them all. It is needless to say that this room is well guarded.

The armory contains a vast collection of armor and arms of all times and countries: goat-skin shields of the barbarians; chain-armor of Japan, China, and the Islands of the Sea; armor of the Crusaders; and steel armor so perfect and complete that one could not be hurt by any art of war known at the time it was used. There is also a great display of horse-armor, all mounted on frames, and looking so lifelike that one almost feels himself in the presence of a corps of twelfth-century knights in line for the fray.

The South Kensington Museum is an extension of the British Museum, though it is ten times as large, and much more elaborate every way than the British Museum proper. One could not see through all its apartments in a week, if he were at all careful to look at things that attracted him. A month, at least, would be required to investigate it thoroughly, while a student could spend months in a single department. One of its buildings is occupied by the Royal Albert Art Collection, one of the largest and finest in the world. I regretted that we could not spend a day more among these wonderful collections; but our time was up, and on Saturday morning we took the train for Liverpool, and resumed our long journey.

We reached Liverpool about three in the afternoon, and found our ship waiting for us.

We were soon aboard; and were shortly joined by the rest of the party, except Dr. West and family, from whom we separated in London. They went by another line to Singapore. But a party of six missionaries of the Dutch Reformed Church joined us at Liverpool. These were led by Dr. Chamberlain, who had been twenty-five years in India. He had also made extensive explorations in the Holy Land. He afforded us all much pleasure and instruction along the voyage.

We sailed at midnight, and Sabbath morning found us suffering from seasickness again. The weather was very bad in the Bay of Biscay. We reached Gibraltar Friday afternoon, and had four hours on shore while they were coaling the ship.

Gibraltar rock is the end of a long, low point of sand, running down into the sea. To the landward from the rock it is so low that one would fancy the sea could flow over it when running high. The rock rises abruptly from the sea to the height of fourteen hundred feet. From the bay it looks like a huge lion, frowning on the Continent of Europe; and when we double the point, and swing out into the Mediterranean, and view it from the east, it looks like two mighty *leos*—one facing north and the other south. The channel is ten miles wide at

Gibraltar, but the English guns so sweep it as to give them entire control of it. On shore is an old Spanish town, with a Moorish castle, and an English town of twenty thousand people. The sides of the rock are fairly honeycombed with batteries, and the artillery galleries are among the finest in the world. The largest guns weigh one hundred tons.

Saturday was beautiful, and we sailed all day in full view of the dark flanks and snow crowns of the Sierra Nevada Mountains of Southern Spain. We had fine weather all the time we were on the Mediterranean. One morning we saw two whales near by, spouting and steaming, and lifting their huge tails ten or twelve feet in the air. We passed Malta and Cyprus in the night; espied Cape Bon one morning, and thought of Carthage and Hannibal and Regulus and the long Punic Wars.

We were eight days on the Mediterranean; and reached Port Said Sabbath morning, entered the Suez Canal, and stopped for coal. Nearly all the missionaries went ashore; but we had scruples, and so did not go. We remained on the ship, and watched the Egyptian Arabs fill the tender with coal. It is a great sight. They coal a ship quicker at Port Said than anywhere else on earth. An officer of our ship told me he had known of their putting eight hundred and fifty tons in a ship in two hours. An immense coal-barge is towed alongside of the ship. Two and sometimes four sets of gang-planks are thrown across. Immediately the shovelers begin filling large, pliable baskets, which hold one hundred pounds each. These the carriers take on the back, between the shoulders, and trot away up the plank. Soon there are two streams of one-hundred-pound loads, as closely together as men can move on a trot, flowing into the ship. They change men every fifteen minutes; and while they were resting many of them ate their breakfasts, which they had brought with them in dirty rags. This meal consisted at best of a rough, brown, unleavened, puffy cake, about as large as a common dinner-plate. They were two or three inches thick in the middle, but made up of two thin crusts and a hollow center. Some of them had pieces of fish, which they put in this hollow, and with onions made a meal; but most of them had no fish. They would break a hole in one side of their cake, and fill it with water. Soon the two crusts became limp and separate; the feaster would roll each of them about one or two onions, and seem to relish them very much. Often they do not have time to finish before they are called on again, and they tuck one roll in a pocket or fold of their dirty clothes, and eat the other as they go with their loads. This breakfast is eaten in the midst of dense clouds of coal-dust, and without washing of face or hands. As soon as their work is done, many of them throw over their shoulders some old blanket or coat, and lie down on the floor, or edge of the barge, and go right to sleep in the sun.

We spent Sunday in the Suez Canal, amid scenes of the greatest interest. Millions of pelicans waded in the shallow waters about the north end of the canal. Here we cross a Jerusalem caravan-road at the ferry. Here is an Arab village, and near it an immense dredging-machine is deepening and broadening the canal. A herd of seventy-five or a hundred camels are laden with big baskets, which the Arabs are filling with sand that has banked up along the edge of the canal. These camels will carry it back to the desert. Here comes a caravan from Egypt to Jerusalem. And away the desert-wastes stretch in every direction, in limitless monotony, save for the enchanting illusion—the mirage—whose lakes and cities and groves are ever fleeing and melting away, and rising in renewed splendor beyond. It was a charmed day to us.

It is very expensive to keep this canal open, and one can readily see why the old canal of the Ptolemys was so often abandoned and reopened. This, the first ship-canal in the world, connected the Nile with the Red Sea, and was at one time ninety-two miles long. It was constructed first by one of the Pharaohs, but merely to convey water. Ptolemy Philadelphus first enlarged it to a ship canal. It was abandoned for a time, and the Emperor Trajan reopened and lengthened it. After the fall of the Roman Empire it again fell into disuse, until Omar, the great Mohammedan, again reopened it, about A. D. 600. Of course this old canal had nothing more to do with the present than to forcibly suggest it, though the part of it south of the Bitter Lakes follows about the same course. The sand is blown and washed in, and fills it continually. The walls last but a short time, and are continually being replaced. The toll paid by our ship for this single passage was about five thousand dollars. The amount is determined partly by the tonnage of the ship, partly by the weight of the cargo, and partly by the number of passengers. The canal is eighty miles long.

We stopped but a few minutes off Suez, at the south end of the canal, Monday morning. We spent the week in the Red Sea till Saturday night. The weather was hot, and, toward the end of the week, boisterous. When we entered the Red Sea a double awning was drawn over the passenger part of the ship, and we spent most of the time on deck. Some of us slept on deck, when there was not too much wind and spray. We came out into the Arabian Sea on Sunday morning, Christmas-day; sighted Aden in the distance, but did not stop. One of the officers told us of an Irishman, who remarked, when he saw this sea town, surrounded by its desolate and 'burning wastes: "And this is Aden? Little wonther Mother Ave was discontinted! Oi 'd ate anything to get out of such a place!" After ten days more of varied experience, much storm and seasickness, we reached Bombay, January 3, 1888.

Chapter III.

FIRST IMPRESSIONS.

WE were met on the ship by Revs. A. W. Prautch; J. E. Robinson, presiding elder of the Bombay District; and Dr. Butcher, the expectant bridegroom. They gave us a hearty welcome, and Brother Prautch helped us greatly in landing. It is difficult for two persons who can not understand each other, to keep from raising the voice in the effort to be understood. There were several missionaries, and Brother Prautch was called here and there to help them. Some of us tried to express our desires to the native cartmen and coachmen without the aid of an interpreter. At different times the eye of some amused looker-on led me to realize that I was throwing my arms in the wildest fashion, and trying to out-yell a great crowd of Coolies and *Ghariwallahs*. It was raining very hard when we landed, an unusual thing for Western India at that season of the year.

We were taken to a hotel, which I suppose was as good as the average in India, but which seemed to us, like everything else, exceedingly filthy. The ground-floor looked and smelt like a cow-stable; indeed, the whole city seemed to us to be pervaded by such an odor.

When we were shown to our room, to our surprise, our bed had no sheets, pillows, or covers on it. We learned, on inquiry, that travelers in India always furnish their own bedding; and no one would think of using bed-clothing in common use as in this country. This is because of the prevalence of skin and other diseases. Even when visiting a friend, one takes his own bedding. We were in a strait; for we had packed our bedding in large boxes, which we could not well get at. But we managed it some way, and retired, only to spend a sorry night fighting bugs. Mrs. Isham had never seen one of these pests, and I really did not know what was annoying us; but we afterward learned that they are so common in India that "bug" means bedbug, and one is so understood when he uses the word. Other bugs are properly called beetles. A gentleman said he had often complained to his landlord of being tormented by bugs at night, and finally the landlord said: "Well, I do n't know what can be done. They are just as bad in my bed as in yours!" And this was in one of the best English hotels in Bombay. They can be kept out only by the most constant care, even in private homes. I have frequently visited in homes of well-to-do people, and seen them in daylight, crawling on drawing-room furniture and on the dress of the lady of the house. We spent but one unhappy night in the hotel, when Dr. Salini Armstrong and her sister, of Nebraska, called, and invited us to share their hospitality while we were detained in Bombay. We gladly accepted, and could not have asked for more comfortable and cleanly quarters and Christian-like entertainment.

No one without experience can realize how powerful and hurtful is the tropical sun. We took every precaution, wore double hats, and carried heavy double umbrellas; and yet, from the first day, Mrs. Isham had sun-headaches, and I had a sun-chill the second night after landing.

We were in Bombay more than three weeks, waiting for the meeting of the South India Conference. This was a time of the greatest trial and temptation. We had nothing to do. The missionaries were all very busy with their work, closing up the year. As we were not going to stay in Bombay, and the language would be different where we were sent, it was useless to begin the study of the language. We went about sight-seeing, and studying the peoples, their customs, and peculiar institutions, as well as we could. Under the most favorable circumstances, the pressure of heathenism is very heavy on the faith of the inexperienced missionary. One feels so alone in the midst of these vast crowds of heathen! He feels that it is almost presumptuous for him to say that he has the true faith, and all these surging thousands are wrong. And then he feels so far away from them. He can not speak their language; he can not make them understand his signs, for their gestures are so different from ours. Theirs are graceful and expressive, and make ours seem stiff and angular. And then, the looks of mingled suspicion, fear, and indifference from those one wishes to help, the frauds he is such an easy victim to, and a thousand other such experiences, have a very cooling effect on his zeal, and rest like mountain-weights upon his faith. It is a new and entirely different experience in the life of the missionary. He begins to realize how many stays and props one has at home to keep him on the way. The support of pastor and brethren in the fellowship of the Church the prevalence, authority, and popularity of Christianity—which give it the sweep of a mighty current to carry one toward faith— and all such kindred helps, are at first very much missed. But all this trial is exceedingly beneficial. The missionary finds himself between Jesus and heathenism, with all its woe and evil;

and, if he be a true Christian, he comes into a much closer fellowship with the Savior than he has ever known before. In the past he has depended so much on the Church and its agencies and fellowships; now he must walk with Christ alone in his spiritual life, and go between Christ and his fellow-man in his life of ministering. One of the weakest points in American Christian character is this lack of independent reliance upon the Savior. Unless we have everything to our taste and everybody agreeable, it is next to impossible for us to work and rejoice; and many of us can do nothing, except when wrought up through some sensational means.

Besides this soul-depression of heathenism, there were at the time peculiar conditions in the work in South India; and considerable dissatisfied and discouraging talk was indulged in by some of the missionaries we met in Bombay. The work in South India had been opened by Bishop Wm. Taylor during his four years' campaign in that country, and had moved forward on the self-support principle until the Conference of 1887, when it was decided to accept the offered subsidies of the Missionary Society. The work was in the transition state when we landed. The Conference of '88 was the twelfth session, and the work was started by Wm.

Taylor in '74; so that there had been fourteen years of the trials and triumphs of self-support before very much help came from America. Hence, the work to this time had been carried on mostly among the English and Eurasians, because they were the only people in India who could be induced to support the work. To our surprise, the missionaries had so completely devoted their time to the English, and had changed about so much, that very few of them had mastered a native language so far as to be able to preach in it; and it did not seem to us that they were any more missionaries than if they were preaching in America.' Furthermore, it was pretty clear that we were to be put at this English work for a time; and this was the sorest of disappointments to us then. But now it is a matter of thanksgiving; for we afterward learned that there is no more important nor directly missionary work in India than this among the English-speaking classes. While engaged in this work, we were supported by the people, and not by American missionary money; so that we do not now have the regret of having put the Missionary Society to a large expense for no service from us. We were not only supported by our Church, but raised five hundred dollars in the two years for missionary work right in the field, and so supported a large native work of schools, Sunday-schools, preaching, and literature work, which we directed through assistants. By going into the English work, we were able to begin at once, and so were useful for the time we were there; while those of our party who were to enjoy the great privilege of remaining steadily in the field were given appointments to the native stations. Whatever may be said *pro* or *con* of self-support as a principle in the world's evangelism, one thing is certainly clear—that, following this principle, Bishop Taylor has committed our Church to a vast work which, in all probability, it would never otherwise have undertaken. And as we see it now, after some experience and observation, we believe it was through God's leading, and not by the choice of man, that this great work has been committed to us as a Church.

On Sundays, while we were waiting, I usually preached once or twice in one of our three English churches in Bombay. I preached my first sermon in the Mazagon Church, and created a little amusement by speaking of the fatality of having one lack. I was preaching on the Savior's words to the rich young man. After the service, a brother remarked that he did not know about America, but in India one *lakh* was considered a good thing to have. *Lakh* means one hundred thousand, and is especially applied to that number of rupees. This error is not so grievous in comparison with some that are made. There are so many words almost identical in sound and form that have very different meanings, that very ludicrous blunders are to be expected of new missionaries. We were told a number of times in India that, for a long time, the doxology was sung in one language, "Praise God from whom all sausages flow," until at last a missionary noticed the error. And a noted missionary told us that, in his early experience, while on a missionary tour, he was giving his cook directions about preparing a meal. He told him, as he thought, to go to the village, and get a fowl and dress it. The cook showed such evident bewilderment that he suspected he had blundered. On inquiry, he found he had told the cook to go to hades, and get a boy and dress it. The natives will very rarely show before one's face that they notice a mistake; but after an interview with a blunderer alone, or with their fellows, they give vent to their amusement.

And so the days went by, and finally we repaired to Poonah to attend the session of Conference. The Conference had then about thirty members. Their physical condition, as registered in their faces, was by no means encouraging. One brother had just recovered from cholera; another was shaking, before our eyes, with a daily malarial chill; two others were about to return to America in shattered health; and, with very few exceptions, every one looked pallid and sick. The contrast in appearance between those of us who had just landed and those who had been years in the field, was, in point of health, strikingly in our favor; but there was no heart-sickness nor spiritual malaria noticeable. Every one was hopeful, buoyant, joyful; and even those who were sick attended the sessions and served on the committees. They were, for the most part, a company of heroes, seasoned and tried amid the privations and vicissitudes of the years of self-support. Most of them are still in the field, and are laying the foundations of Christ's kingdom broad and strong to save the millions. I would rather have a humble place in their ranks than to enjoy all the comforts and associations and honors American life affords.

We were entertained at the home of Rev. Mr. Sorabjee, a converted Parsee, and a minister of the Church of England. Of course there were some things in the home customs and manners of these native people that were strange to us, but we were never more royally entertained. Mr. Sorabjee was absent, but his cultured wife and daughters left nothing undone that we could have asked for. Each member of the family was engaged directly in missionary, evangelistic, or educational work. One of the daughters was the first lady in the Bombay Presidency to receive the B. A. degree. She had been presented to the queen; and the mother had traveled and lectured in England, and raised large sums of money for mission-work. But there was not the slightest show made of these things, nor any ostentation in anything. This was a model home; the Bible was thoroughly studied daily, privately and in the family circle; and no one can estimate the influence for good exerted in the midst of heathenism by such devoted and active lives.

Mrs. Sorabjee arranged for us to take tea at the home of a wealthy Parsee widow—Mrs. Wadai. Here we met only ladies: the mother, wearing the white cap of widowhood, and her beautiful and graceful daughters. The house was large, and richly furnished, though quite differently from an American mansion. The floor and walls were marble, the latter being decorated, in each room, by life-size paintings of the deceased head of the family. We had a very delicate and delicious tea, at which Madam Wadai presided with all the dignity and grace of the first lady of the land. After tea she cou-ducted us through the house, bringing us at last to her own private study—an airy and delicately ornamented little room. She drew out a secret drawer in her secretary, and showed us her Bible, which we well knew from her conversation she had been studying, though secretly, for fear of her people. This Bible had found its way into this home, and its light to the hearts of these women, through the patient influence of good Mother Sorabjee. Mrs. Wadai was very wealthy, having three other splendid mansions, at different altitudes, enabling her to live in a delightful climate the year round. When we left she gave us her photograph, which we still prize very highly.

Through the kindness of Brother Prautch, I got to visit the high-priest of all the Parsee fire-temples of the Deccan, who resides in the winter in Poonah. He lives in a splendid mansion, surrounded by a very park of drives and ornamental shrubbery. He received us very cordially, having met Mr. Prautch once before in a railway carriage. He showed us through his great house, seating us at last in his large library. He had all sorts of books—mostly English—and prominent among them was the Holy Bible. I finally succeeded in getting the conversation directed to religion. He told me of the excellence of the moral principles of the religion of Zoroaster. These, he said, were briefly summarized and stated: "Pure thoughts, pure words, and good deeds." When I asked him how we sinful creatures were to meet these high requirements, he had little to say. I attempted to impress upon him that this was one point, at least, where the religion of Jesus is superior to every other. Though its spiritual requirements are the very highest, yet it affords us the needed help to attain them. He had, very likely, had the same thing said to him many times, and it did not seem to strike him with any particular force. He was the headman of his religion for a great district; he derived his sumptuous support from its revenues; and naturally enough he would be very slow to recognize the superiority of what, to him, seems like conquering robbery. At last he said, half-mournfully: "In one hundred and fifty years there will be no Parsees. Our people are rapidly becoming Europeans. Already they have adopted your dress, your education, and many of your customs and ways of thinking. The revenues of our temples are declining, our people are weakening in their devotion to their ancient religion, and soon they will become Christians." One could hardly fail to be touched with sympathy for this brother's feelings; and yet it would be unchristian not to pray, in the interests of these very people, "God speed the day!"

These Parsees are a remnant of the ancient Persians. Their religion is so ancient that its founder was a mythical personage before Christianity was born. There are perhaps but about a hundred thousand of these people in India, of which fifty thousand are in Bombay. They are a very thrifty, and hence a very wealthy, community, and are often called "the Yankees of India." Their ancestors came to India centuries ago, on being expelled by the Mohammedan conquerors of their own land. They are very intelligent, speak English fluently, and are usually courteous and helpful to strangers. They have some of the filthiest of religious practices—such, for instance, as drinking cow's urine while warm. They expose their dead to the vultures on the Tower of Silence, below which is a large and deep well, to which the bones are consigned after being stripped of their flesh. At Bombay this Tower of Silence is situated on Malabar Hill, in the midst of the most beautiful garden,

> "Where every prospect pleases,
> And only man is vile."

But on the streets and tram-cars, and in the marts, the Parsee appears as the neatest in person, the richest in dress, and the most courteous and business-like in manner of any of the native people.

Our Conference was presided over by the saintly George Bowen, for forty years a missionary in India, mostly in Bombay. Brother Bowen was the least self-assertive, the lowliest and meekest soul I ever met. He said very little; but I, at least, was charmed in his presence. I knew nothing of him before going to India. Brother Frease took me to call on him in Bombay. I greeted him as "Father Bowen;" for he looked like a patriarch, if any man ever did. He quietly and emphatically corrected me. "Not Father, but Brother Bowen," he said. He turned the conversation at once; but I should never have dared to call him father again. He began inquiring for our health, and prescribed for our headache. The second Sunday we were in Bombay, I was to preach in our Grant Road Church. Dinner was late where we were stopping, and I was five minutes late in getting to the church. During the next week, Brother Bowen came to the hospital to hold a Bible-class with the servants. As soon as he saw me, he said in the quietest, kindest tone, "You were late Sunday night." I had not thought of it before, except to shift the blame; but I now felt stung to the very heart. I began to say, "The servants were late with dinner," when, in the gentlest and yet most authoritative voice, he said: "You are in the King's business; you must never be late!" This word had such power that I have never been late since; and I never think of being late that they do not ring in my ears. Again, when we were boarding the train to go to Poonah—there were a number of the missionaries and their families, and the separate apartments for Europeans are limited—and every one was scrambling to get in, this lame and weak and aged saint called to me that, if I would hand him his carpet-bag, he would find room elsewhere. I do not believe there was a missionary who noticed it that did not blush for his own selfishness. For my own part, I never see selfishness manifested on the cars that I do not think of Brother Bowen; and it is my study to act less like a dog in a manger, to say the least, than if I had not learned of him. He presided in this Conference when he was so feeble he could hardly sit up or speak audibly to those distant from him; and yet, by the power of his presence, the brethren, though the conflict of interest and opinion was sharp, were kept within the bounds of good order. But a few days after this Conference, this man of God—sainted in the estimation of both heathen and Christian—breathed out his life upon the wings of a beautiful tropical morning, and entered into rest. He lived wonderfully near the gospel standard of carelessness for the things of this world, and of devotion to seeking first the kingdom of God. Many are the stories of his practicing the letter, as well as the spirit, of the Sermon on the Mount. Once a native man was running away with his coat, when he called to him to let him take some valuable papers—valueless to the thief—from the pocket, before he took the coat away. He did not demand the coat, nor even censure the man for taking it; and the thief was so astonished and shamed that he brought it back. At another time, he entertained the Bombay Missionary Conference. This body, since Bombay is a city of near a million people, and the headquarters of many mission agencies, is a dignified company of, perhaps, two hundred missionaries from most denominations and Protestant lands. Their custom was to have their session about eight o'clock, and take breakfast afterward with the missionaries who entertained them. The spread on such an occasion would be apt to be rather elaborate anywhere in Christendom. But Brother Bowen furnished the Conference with merely bread and bananas—his own accustomed breakfast, only on a larger scale. But when he went to eat with another, he had no criticism to offer on the home arrangements or the food, but ate without remark what was set before him. He is said to have frequently remarked that he did not know of one soul who had been led to Christ through his agency; but missionaries, and many others of all classes of society, bear a different testimony to the results of his life's labor. He furnishes a striking example of the truth of Spurgeon's statement: "The most powerful influence on earth, aside from the Spirit of God himself, is the serene and quiet beauty of a holy life."

When the appointments were announced, we found our work was the pastorate of the English Church in Madras. I had talked with Dr. Rudisill—who had been pastor there for three years, and was presiding elder of the Madras District—and was perfectly willing to go with him to the work assigned. As soon as I saw him, my soul knit to him, and all misgivings were of the past. The prospect of getting to work in a field of our own also relieved the pressure; and altogether, we were glad we were in India by the close of the Conference. The Madras missionaries traveled in a party, taking the train about nine o'clock in the evening. We were thirty-four hours on the way—reaching Madras, without change of cars, on the morning of the second day. Dr. A. W. Rudisill, Rev. A. H. Baker, and

Miss Grace Stephens, of Madras; and Miss M. A. Hughes—daughter of the editor of the *Guide to Holiness*, of New York, and the first missionary sent by the Woman's Foreign Missionary Society to the Madras District—and ourselves, constituted the party. The trip across India was full of surprises to us. It was made in comparative comfort. We missionaries had a compartment to ourselves the most of the time, and we used it religiously and joyfully. I realized afterward that I was under kindly and hopeful inspection by my presiding elder and Brother B. as to theology, peculiarities, and disposition; but it was so indirect that I did not notice it. A person with a bad disposition, and hard to get on with, is more of a nuisance than anything else in a mission-field. Ill-nature is more harmful there than elsewhere, and there is considerable suspense until the new missionary is found to be agreeable. And it not infrequently happens that a tolerably decent disposition here at home becomes utterly unbearable in missionary life. We reached Madras about seven A. M., were met at the station by Mrs. Rudisill, our presiding elder's wife, and were soon seated at breakfast with the whole party in the parsonage where we were to live.

Chapter IV.

AT WORK.

MADRAS is a city of four hundred thousand people. It has a purely European population of about four thousand, and a Eurasian—that is, mixed European and Asiatic—population of probably fourteen thousand. This latter community speaks the English language, and their habits of life are as nearly like those of the English as their income and education make possible. They are all nominally Christians; and, considering that most of them are brought up closely associated with the heathen peoples about them, and where the most of the Christianity they see is either of the Romish or the ritualistic sort, they make a fairly successful showing religiously. We all know how difficult it was for God to keep the Hebrew people from falling into the ways of the heathen about them; and one can hardly overestimate the power of surrounding heathenism to tempt and ensnare lustful humanity. If it were possible for the heathenism of India or China to transplant its worship and its abominations in the midst of

American society, it would not require two generations to pass till a majority of the people would be corrupted to a greater or less degree. But these Eurasians, with the sprinkling of full-blood English Christians who mingle and worship with them, are becoming more and more a recognized and powerful factor for the evangelization of India. Bishop Wm. Taylor's coming, with a foresight which seems almost prophetic, and his four years' campaign of revival-work among the East Indians, was the beginning of a new religious era for them. Bishop Taylor's theory was, that the heathen could never be converted with a dead, formal Church of merely nominal Christians in the way. His thought was to thoroughly arouse this existing body of English and Eurasian Christians, that they might exhibit the triumphs and joys of salvation, and be enlisted under the power of the Holy Ghost to evangelize their own land, and thus a mighty hindering force would be turned into an indigenous missionary force. His theory has proven correct, but its reduction to practice has gone on slower than he probably anticipated; and this because it is difficult to find enough men of the zeal and physical endurance necessary to thoroughly evangelize the Christian body. Yet a great work in this direction has been going on ever since his day there, and many of our very best missionary workers are from this class.

Our Church consisted almost entirely of Eurasians. They paid us one hundred and fifty rupees—about fifty dollars—a month; own their own church and parsonage; and paid, during our pastorate, twenty-five dollars a month for native work.

We soon found our work was going to tax us to the utmost. Besides our large church in Vepery, we had two small mission-chapels, in one of which I preached once a week, and occasionally in the other. Each had a Eurasian Sunday-school. Then we soon opened three day-schools and four Sunday-schools among the natives, conducted by native teachers under my supervision. Besides this, there was our Publishing-house in Madras, which was working then in three languages, and employing from thirty to forty men, including the book-binding department. This was an almost entirely self-supporting institution, doing job-work for banks and colleges and missions, and requiring to be so run as to give a profit with which to turn out Sunday-school and other mission literature. One can imagine some of the difficulties met, and annoying, time-consuming details, in suiting the exact Englishman, with careless, inexact printers, and without experience himself. But shortly after we reached Madras, Dr. Rudisill had to go to Bangalore, to take charge of the work there; and, besides all my preaching and other work, I had to take charge of this press. I found I had never known what it was to work. Withal, I tried to study Tamil, and progressed so far as to be able to read and write a little; and studied up on the Conference-course studies, as in America. This overloading could not be helped, as there was no one to share the work with me. I worked so hard and constantly that I contracted dyspepsia, and could hardly digest milk and toast the last months we were in Madras. I was green, as is almost every new recruit, and doubt not that I expended much energy unnecessarily.

My good wife soon found her hands more than full. The Church may be made to furnish to these Eurasian people religious life, social life, literary life. Mrs. Isham held a social at the parsonage once every month or two. She organized an Oxford League—the forerunner of the Epworth—the first one in India. Through it she led the young people in their devotional life, and to engage in various literary exercises. The League is still a strong and useful society in the Vepery Church. And then came her missionary society for the ladies, and her catechism-class for the children, and the care of the home, and the study of the language, and the thousand nameless details of social and religious visiting and ministering to the sick; all this, and, if she could get any time, she would help me read proof for the *Press*, and post the mission-books, and pay and instruct the teachers of our native schools, and the like. I give these details that my readers may know that their missionaries are the fullest of care and the hardest of workers.

And right here I may write of the dangers that confront the new missionary: First, he will break himself down with overwork; second, he will not protect himself sufficiently against the dangers of the climate; and, third, he will undertake so much work that he has neither the money nor the strength to do it well. Really, for the first two years, if not for five, where his work lies among the heathen, his principal effort is spent on himself, and not on the heathen. He must learn the language, the etiquette, and many other things about the people, and get himself as well seasoned as possible to stand the climate. He will be in danger of becoming too serious and intense. He must never forget that joy is his strength; and the heavier his burdens, and the more desolate his surroundings, the more joyful he needs to be. He needs to learn well how to keep his heart a fountain of joy.

The returned missionary is so often asked, "Did you like it over in India?" And one must say in sum total, "Yes," and very decidedly, too. In what does this liking consist? In the fascination of the work; because, often, of its foundation character; and because it needs so much to be done, and there is no one else but the missionary to do it. There is no sense sweeter to the soul than that of being useful to Jesus in ministering for him to those he died to save. At home here, the returned missionary so often feels that, if the earth should swallow up his church-building and himself some night, humanity could get on about as well. It might create a little flurry for a time with a few; but the other Churches could easily and gladly take care of the flock; and none need go to eternity without gospel light.

As the season advanced, the heat became very trying. Almost every one breaks out with heat-rash, which is extremely nettling; and when one is annoyed with all he can bear in his work, he is apt to become petulant. There is a general exodus of the English from the plains to the hills at this season; and all who can take a short respite from the period of extremest heat—which, in Southern India, is from May

15th to June 15th—do so. We went this first year, for a short time, to Bangalore, in the hills on the eastern side of the interior elevation, about two hundred miles west of Madras. Dr. and Mrs. Rudisill, Brother Baker and family, and W. L. King and family, were in charge of the various branches of the work there at the time. Mrs. Rudisill came down with typhoid fever, and for forty-seven days her life hung in the balance. She had lived three years in Madras, and it is likely that the change to the colder climate of the hills brought on the fever. The missionaries of all denominations in Madras and vicinity joined in praying for her recovery, and those who know the case and circumstances have no doubt but that God raised her up in answer to these prayers.

Chapter V.

A LETTER FROM THE FIELD.

I WISH to let the reader have a view of life in India, and I can do no better than give the contents of a circular letter written during our first year.

"Many things are different from our fancies before we came. There are many more of the facilities and comforts of civilization than we had supposed. We have daily papers, with telegraphic news from Europe and America, railways which make travel cheap and fairly comfortable, and an excellent mail and postal telegraph system. The postman comes to our house twice a day. Foreign mail comes regularly once a week. There are so many English people that, except for one's work and servants, he need have nothing to do with the natives. There are excellent English stores, where we can buy almost anything we could in European markets. American canned meats, and fruits fresh from California, and crackers in air-tight tins from London and New York, as fresh as when they came from the baker's oven, can be had quite reasonably. Labor is so cheap that clothing can be had much cheaper than in either America or England. The gents' tailors and fitters are Mohammedans. They do very well, if one refuses to pay them till he is satisfied. A suit that would cost $40 in America can be gotten for $20 or $25 in India, but not so well made.

"Americans who have not taken the pains to inform themselves are apt to think of India as covered with dense forests and luxurious vegetation, abounding in elephants and tigers and big snakes, and peopled with naked natives who never saw a white man. So it is quite a surprise to one full of such fancies to find a country the most of which, during most of the year, looks like a desert, to rarely hear of a wild animal larger or more fierce than the yelping jackal, or of reptiles much larger than the American blacksnake. It is true that the deadly cobra is very numerous, and it is said that fifty thousand natives die from his bite in a single year in the province of Bengal alone. But this worst of serpents is a timid creature, and I never heard of a European or an American being bitten by one. The missionaries sometimes have very harrowing experiences with them, because they so frequently come into the houses, and hang themselves upon door-knobs, nails, clothes-racks, and stretch out on window-sills, and so on; but it usually happens that both the snake and the missionary escape unharmed; for their fear is mutual. We never saw but one cobra, except those carried about by the jugglers; and it crawled into my study in the middle of a very hot day, evidently in quest of a cool place. Mrs. Isham was resting a short time on a lounge beside my study-table. She lay still while it crawled past her twice. I sat writing at my table. She whispered, 'There is a snake.' I looked up, and in a low tone said, 'It's a cobra, too.' It heard my voice, and turned back upon itself quickly, and was gone before we could trace it. I called some men over from the *Press*. They dug up the brick and cement doorstep, and killed it with a crowbar before it could disentangle itself.

"The Englishman dominates everything in India. It matters not what his character is, or his real merit—he is, in appearance at least, held in high respect by the natives. They will rarely sit in his presence, and call him master, or *sahib*, which means gentleman. There is a larger number of English in India than is generally supposed in America. They are, for the most part, employed in Government, military, and civil service. Their incomes are large, and they live in elaborate style, as a rule.

"All India now—June 5th—is parched, and

as barren as a desert. Green spots occur only by thorough irrigation, and the water must be drawn from wells for this purpose. In large cities, like Bombay and Madras, the Government provides a plentiful supply of water by collecting it in artificial reservoirs, and conducting it often many miles. But in most of the towns the water is carried from large pools on the heads of Coolies, or drawn by an ox in a barrel-cart, or carried in large leather sacks on the backs of oxen. A sack of this kind is made of the whole hide of a goat or calf. Water is precious now, and vile, in most parts of this burning land. Its two hundred and eighty millions of people, with all their fields and flocks and herds, require a vast quantity of water. Here, at Madras, we are thirteen degrees from the equator, and six feet below the level of the sea. The sun stands a little to the north of us at noon, and will do so for two months to come. We shall be under the almost direct rays of the sun for six months of the year. The most careful precautions must be taken now against sunstroke. Our hats are one and a half inches thick, and we carry double umbrellas, covered with white. But it is said to be the healthiest season of the year.

"We are furnished with a good English brougham. Our horse is one of my own choosing—a flea-bitten-gray Persian mare, the toughest and best of horses to be had in India. If she is driven ten miles one day, she must rest all the next. Horses are not taken out in the middle of the day unless absolutely necessary, and then they are often provided with solar *topes*—that is, a shade, made of pith, for the head, neck, and loins. The average time of usefulness for horses is three or four years. After that their wind is gone. If the climate has such an effect on horses, one can see why it is such a trial to the health of Americans to live here.

"And how do we keep cool in the house? We do just the reverse of what we should do in America. There we should open the windows and doors; but here we shut up everything, at eight or nine in the morning, except two or three windows and a door on the side of the house from which the wind comes. Over these we hang *cus-cus tatties*—that is, a curtain woven like a rag-carpet, only more loosely. The woof is of fine yellow roots; the warp is of strong hemp cord. These are wet every half-hour or so; and as the wind blows through them it is cooled, dampened, and perfumed by the odor of the roots, which is quite pleasant. The feeling on going from the outside into a room so cooled, is not unlike that on going into a cellar, on a hot summer day, in America. But, with the temperature so reduced, it is often necessary to keep a thick blotting-paper under the hand, to protect the paper from perspiration stains, while writing.

"Besides this, a *punkah* is kept swinging overhead to keep the air in motion. A *punkah* consists of a heavy board, about six inches wide, and from six to twelve feet long. This is suspended from the ceiling by neatly covered ropes. On both sides of the lower edge of this plank is suspended a heavy plaited frill of cloth, about eighteen inches wide. This frill is made of coarse stiff cloth, covered and lined with linen, and otherwise ornamented, so that, when properly made, they relieve the barn-like appearance of the necessarily large and high rooms, and when properly swung create a good breeze.

"In America it is expensive to keep warm; but here, to keep cool. Six months in the year these *punkahs* must be swung while we sleep, and while we work in the study. We employ two men to pull them at night, and a boy for the day. We pay each of these pullers a dollar a month. It may be surprising to some that this is their entire income, and they board themselves. The men very likely support others, and their entire income will be not more than four cents a day. They sit just outside the house, and swing the *punkah* by a rope, which passes through a hole in the wall and over a pulley.

"This brings us easily to speak of the servants it is necessary to keep, in order to live and work in India. We sometimes hear from globe-trotting tourists a sight of criticism on the fact that missionaries support so large an establishment. It does seem strange to you in America that we, for instance, keep thirteen servants; but the strangeness comes from one's utter inability to take in the situation without the experience of keeping a house in India. In the first place, it is the law of the Missionary Society that the missionary and his wife shall give their whole time and strength to missionary work. And this is a very wise rule; for it does not pay to send cultured American women over here to do housework, when women can be gotten here for a dollar and a half a month to do it. We Americans are almost foolishly committed to the thinking that a woman who does no housework does nothing. This notion is peculiar to Americans, and inspires us with an unreasoning contempt for housekeeping by the servant system. We should remember that it is waste of labor and money to put skilled and expensive workmen at cheap and common employments. Let every one work, and let him work at the highest work he can do well.

"Then, it would cost almost any American woman her life to attempt to cook and do housework here; and she could not do it so well with the rude appliances as do the natives to the manner born. It is necessary for us to have many servants, because the iron laws of caste prevent one servant from doing more than one sort of work. The cook who does the marketing must not carry the basket nor fetch the water. The *ayah* who cares for the children must not sweep the floor. The man who cares for the horse must not care for the yard and water the plants. So it is necessary for us to keep the thirteen here in Madras, to get along and be free to work for the Church. No one feels worse about this than the missionaries, for it is a great annoyance to manage all these servants and to keep them from cheating us out of everything. The cost of keeping them is not as much as of keeping one good girl in America. We pay the whole number less than fourteen dollars a month, and they board themselves. We pay this out of our own salary of fifty dollars a month less than the average preacher in America gets, and give our own entire time and strength to the Church. And then these poor people would come to want if some one did not employ them.

This is their only means of keeping soul and body together. They come and beg us to employ them, and attempt to bow down and kiss one's foot in token of their servant spirit; and one would feel condemned to rob the Church of his time and the starving of his bread to save a dollar a month. New missionaries are sometimes disposed to head a revolution on this line; but they succumb with increase of experience. The missionaries who have been long in the field may be trusted both as to devotion and wisdom, for it takes a good deal of both to keep one at his post.

"Of course it is a great event when a missionary is privileged to entertain an American traveler; and there is often more or less of a spread made from the slim purse for the household expenses, which must be paid for by reducing the expenses for some days to come. And the weary worker is apt to lay off, and show his guest about the place in the mission conveyance. Of course, when he has gone to all this trouble, he appreciates the gratitude shown by his guest in thoroughly misrepresenting him where it will do him and his cause the most harm.

"One is surprised that the missionary so little minds the things he imagined would be so horrible to him. There are little lizards everywhere on the walls and ceilings. They make one squeamish at first; and I know one lady missionary who says she put in her first night throwing her shoes at the creatures she saw running about the walls of her room. But one soon learns that these innocent little creatures are good friends, and not half so pestersome as the flies and other insects they destroy would be. Occasionally a scorpion is found about the house; but it rarely happens that one gets stung by one; and, if he does, it is usually because he forgets that he is in a land where such things abound, and so becomes careless. Bandicoots twice the size of a rat, blind mice, and stinking little muskrats, run about the floors freely at night; and sometimes cats will break out into a wild scream under one's bed at midnight. These things afford amusement, and break the monotony of life; and one survives, and works away."

Chapter VI.

AN IMPORTANT EVENT.

THE subject above refers to the conversion of Raju Naidu, which took place during the fall of our first year in Madras. I do not wish to claim him as in any way the fruit of my labors; but as I frequently talked with him during the weeks which preceded his baptism, and had a part in all the experiences which followed it, I may be able to so account for it that my readers will see more clearly than they do now what it means for a man of caste and position in the Hindoo community to become openly a Christian.

Raju Naidu belonged to one of the leading high-caste families in Madras. The family estate was large, and some of his near relatives were high in professional and official standing. He himself had a good position on the staff of a Hindu semi-weekly paper printed in English. He was fairly well educated, speaking three languages; one of which was English, which he used fluently. He was married, and, after the custom of India, lived with his mother and brothers and sisters, his father being dead. This placed his wife and his property more under the control of his family than of himself. Property is held by the family, and not by the individual, as in this country; and, in everything, the family rules, and individuality of thought and action is suppressed. A man may be well off in the family, but, if he goes forth from it, be utterly penniless. And by the education of the girls from their infancy, no high-caste woman can exercise the moral courage to go out, even with her husband, where other men will see her; and her caste will be broken in baptism and communing with Christians; for she is taught that such sins might cost the life of her husband, and ruin her entire family.

So for Raju to become a Christian required that he should absolutely forsake houses and lands and mother and brethren and wife and position, and escape for his eternal life from all these entanglements.

Raju had gone to a mission-school when a boy, and there received his first impressions about Christianity. He had been more or less in touch with missionaries and Christian teaching all along the years. Two or three years before, he had formed the acquaintance of Dr. Rudisill; and Miss Grace Stephens, the zenana missionary of our Church in Madras, had been teaching some of the women in his home, and he had often talked with her, and heard her lessons to the others. All these influences were laying the foundation of his convictions, and unconsciously he was steadily moving toward conversion to Christ.

A municipal election was held in June, and some friend or relative of Raju's was running for commissioner—or alderman, as we say in America. Raju and a friend came in a carriage to take me to vote. Raju returned with me alone, and conversed quite freely concerning his religious views and convictions. At first, he said, he was a zealous Hindu. Then, as his education advanced, he lost all faith in idolatry, and became an Atheist. As time wore on, he saw that a universe of law and providence requires an intelligent designer, who rules in its affairs, and so became a Deist. "And now," said he, "I see that men are helpless in sin, and must have a Savior; I believe Jesus Christ is that Savior, but it costs so much to fully accept him." It is a common thing for the missionary to hear heathen gentlemen speak patronizingly of Christianity; and, for all this brother talked more to the point than they do generally, I doubted whether he meant more than to make himself agreeable to me. I encouraged him all I could, showing him that, though the cost was great, the promised return was a hundred-fold in this life, and eternal life in that which is to come. "The kingdom of God comes not with observation;" and no one can tell, in the mission-fields or at home, whether a seeker is in earnest or not. But the true soul-winner must encourage and help every one; sow among the stones, by the wayside, and among thorns, as well as in what seems to be the fruitful field; for we preach the gospel to win souls, and also as a witness. Three or four months later, Raju visited me, and as I talked with him I realized that he was passing through a life-and-death soul-struggle. Shortly afterward Dr. Rudisill told us he was to be baptized in two or three weeks. During these weeks Raju visited me often; and I have never witnessed a more heroic fight of faith than that he waged against the world, the flesh, and the devil. His face grew thin, his cheeks hollow, and his eyes sunken. He could not eat; he could not sleep. Once, with crying and tears, he said: "I love my wife and mother very dearly; how can I separate from them?" And then, after a moment of quiet, he said: "But I have a soul to save, and what shall it profit me if I gain the whole world and lose it? My wife will be a widow but the few years of this life; but if I lose my soul, it is lost forever. I must leave all for Christ!"

We arranged all the preliminaries for his baptism. The missionaries and native Christians were invited. It was to take place in our Vepery church. About noon of the day appointed, Raju came into my study by the side-door, with two changes of clothes under his arm, and a little money in his purse—everything else of this world being left behind. He had to escape secretly, explaining to his folks that he was going on a little visit. We talked and prayed together; Dr. Rudisill and the other missionaries came in; a little lunch was served, and Raju ate with us, thereby breaking his caste; then we removed his long hair—called *kudimi*—which is religiously regarded in South India, and is one of the marks of the Hindu faith; then we went to the church, and Raju was baptized. Immediately he took the train, with Dr. Rudisill, for Gulbarga, one of our mission-stations in the Deccan, two hundred miles from Madras, where Brother J. H. Garden was then stationed.

His relatives followed him, and we found that Brother Garden was not going to be able to keep them from taking him away. So we determined to bring him back to Madras, and have the struggle through. Dr. Rudisill went after him; and I had handbills printed in three languages, and scattered all over the city—especially in his home neighborhood—stating that Raju Naidu, recently baptized to Christianity, would speak in the Methodist Episcopal Church, Vepery, on Sunday morning at ten o'clock. The distributers of these notices were roughly handled in some instances, and would have been mobbed but for the police.

It was the plan of Raju's friends to meet him at the station, and never let him get to the church. They were there in great numbers; but we had anticipated such a move, and I sent the Church-carriage to Perambore—a suburban station—so that Dr. Rudisill and Raju arrived safely at the parsonage about the time his friends were disappointed at the Central Station. The time for service arrived, and for once we had a large native congregation. The church was packed, and the people were orderly. Dr. Rudisill preached through an interpreter; some Tamil lyrics were sung by the native Christians; then Raju stood up, within a week of his baptism, to explain to his friends and relatives the reasons which impelled him to take the step. He spoke quite confidently, and they listened attentively; but as soon as the service was ended, they broke straight for Raju. I was expecting this, and hurried him over to the parsonage. In a minute nearly the whole crowd of natives, some of them boisterous and angry, were rushing through our house. Dr. Rudisill, the zenana missionaries, and a few of the members of our English Church, were with us; and for more than an hour we baffled this crowd, and finally they departed, leaving Raju with us.

Then we ate a lunch, and lay down to rest a little. In the afternoon, Raju's wife and mother came and prostrated themselves on our veranda, and wailed in token of their bereavement and desolation. Raju wisely refused to see them. They begged that they might merely see his face. They would stay on the outside and look through the glass door, they promised; but Raju would not even grant this. In this he set an example for all young converts; viz., that of avoiding temptation. The Hindus have a superstition that they get power over a person by looking upon his face. Raju knew that one of his battles would be with superstition, and carefully avoided everything that might strengthen this enemy.

For two months Raju's friends tried in many ways to get him in their power; but he successfully avoided them until they gave him up. Had they gotten him away from us, we should probably never have seen him again; but by our protecting and helping him awhile, he was enabled to overcome their opposition, and live and preach and write for Christ among them. He devoted himself to lecturing and writing independent of missionary support. Recently he is on the editorial staff of the *Eastern Star*, and will, if he lives, exert a powerful influence as a Christian layman for Christ and civilization through the years to come.

One can not estimate the far-reaching results of such a missionary victory. It means far more than a revival with five hundred converts does in a Christian land. It sets agoing lines of influence which will affect thousands for Christ, and will go on increasing and blessing generations who will never hear of the missionary whose faith and toil gave God a means of revealing himself to the lost.

Chapter VII.

MOVING FORWARD.

OCTOBER 15th was looked forward to, in our home at least, with longing expectation. It is the day appointed by the Government for the breaking of the eastern monsoon. We had been ten months in Madras, and had seen no rain to speak of. We had endured the long half-year of extreme hot weather, culminating in the sultry heat and heavy air of September and early October. At this time, the atmosphere seems to weigh tons, and makes one's shoulders tired to move about, and his chest tired in supporting respiration. It is like the still, sultry air which precedes the breaking of a summer thunderstorm here in America, lengthened out through two months. And it is with great joy that we greet the ides of October; for the British Government has fixed that date for the rains to begin. The seas about are swept by terrific storms, and navigation is discouraged by the Government as far as it has any influence. The flags are taken down from the harbor-staff; the made harbors, like the one at Madras, are pronounced unsafe; and generally the off season has set in. The Government prognosticates with precision. We had very grave doubts about the rain setting in; for Americans are schooled to be skeptics on this line by the uncertainty and fickleness of all the weather they have known. But at six o'clock sharp on the morning of October 15th the rain began to fall in torrents. There was not the usual preliminary of a sprinkle, or scatttering drops; it was just what it is called—"the burst of the monsoon." It poured down, too, for three days, with but little cessation. Everything was flooded. The surface of the earth became a waste of waters. But as soon as the rain ceased, the water subsided, the earth was dressed in green, and all nature was transformed. It is almost startling to see how quickly the surrounding country changes from a burning desert to the luxurious dress of tropical vegetation.

We were so hungry for the rain and the refreshing sea-air that we did little the first day but watch the water pour down, and enjoy the refreshing. The rain cools the air, washes everything clean; and, with its coming, everything and everybody awake to a new life. About two weeks after this first downpour, the second of the three big rains came. It was a terrific storm—a veritable cyclone. The streets were filled with broken trees, blown up and torn to pieces; wall fences were blown down everywhere; many native huts and some large English houses fell in; and roofs of public buildings were blown off. The sea was as wild and grand a spectacle as one could wish to behold. Fortunately no ships were in the harbor and none near the coast, or they would have been dashed to pieces. One fall there were five splendid ships wrecked at Madras in a similar storm. One was lifted ashore, and left there. All the passengers and sailors, except those who were saved by the throwing of the life-line from the pier, were lost. All Madras was flooded. The water was said to be four feet deep in some of the leading streets. Business was suspended. Many could not get to their offices or work; and many who did, could not get home. After this there was another three days' rainfall; and in these three storms the bulk of the annual rainfall—about fifty-three inches—descended. From this time on till the next April life in Madras is quite pleasant as far as climate is concerned. Our work increased as the year drew to a close; but we were well, and enjoyed it. In January a little stranger, whom we call Robert, came to us; and a week later the father of this new arrival posted off to Bombay to Conference.

The trip required forty hours, and though it was in the dead of winter, I found it necessary during the day to wrap a moistened towel about my head to prevent headache from the sun as we crossed the Deccan. When we awoke, the second morning, we were at Lanowli, at the summit of the Western Ghats. We made the descent as the morning sun was crowning the peaks with gold, and then flooding the valleys with beauty. A more restful and refreshing experience I have never had. After the long, hot year of hard work in flat and sickly Madras, what a change it was to awake, one bright morning, in mountain air and amid mountain scenery, on the way to meet the brethren in Conference, and enjoy the strengthening and rest of a week of fellowship! Still there was a thought of regret through it all, and that was of my sick wife in Madras; cared for truly with skill and tenderness, but by strangers. She could not share in all 'this change and rest. And so it ever is—the weight of monotony, suffering, and sacrifice, rests heaviest on woman.

This was Bishop Thoburn's first year as bishop, and he was everywhere received by missionaries and people with great joy. He presided over the Conference. Bishop Fowler was present—coming by way of Japan, Corea, and

China—and lectured and took part in the platform and other meetings. This will ever be a memorable Conference to me, for here I was ordained under the missionary rule—taking deacon's and elder's orders the same day.

The Conference over, we returned to our fields of labor, strengthened and with new zeal and inspiration. Bishop Thoburn visited Madras immediately after Conference. We had a reception for him at our home, which was attended by two hundred of our Eurasian people. The bishop lectured and preached, and studied every branch of the work. The week following we all went to Bangalore with Bishop Thoburn, and the missionaries and their helpers from the other points, to organize the Madras District Conference. Here the bishop worked in the Conference in the daytime, and preached to the people at night. One who has not seen him in the field would hardly believe, if told, the amount of work the missionary bishop of India accomplishes. But the work is as nothing compared to the burden and care of the work.

The morning after we arrived in Bangalore, a telegram was forwarded to me from Madras. It was for Bishop Thoburn, from Calcutta, and brought the overwhelming intelligence of the sudden death of the Rev. Frank Latimer McCoy, D. D., one of the most promising missionaries our Church ever sent to India. At the time of his death, Dr. McCoy was carrying four men's work. He was manager of the Publishing-house in Calcutta, which was extremely burdensome; for it was in debt about five times the value of its plant. He was principal of the Calcutta Boys' School, a self-supporting boarding-school. He was editor of the *Indian Witness*, the sixteen-page weekly official organ of our Church in India. And he was the presiding elder of the Calcutta District. Bishop Thoburn had a strong personal attachment to Dr. McCoy, as he has to all the missionaries who are associated with him in his great work; and with his sorrow came the fact that four very important posts in the capital of the empire were made vacant, and there was no one but himself, with the care of all the vast work, to take charge of them till they could be manned. On reading the telegram he seemed as if he were stunned by a heavy blow; but he soon took up the work of the day, and showed no signs of being weighed down. He could not stay with us through the Conference, but hastened away to Calcutta to take up the reins that Dr. McCoy had laid down forever. Brother F. W. Warne, pastor of the large English Church, had been so overloaded with work during Dr. McCoy's sickness that he was taken dangerously ill, and had to go for a change to the hills. Bishop Thoburn stepped into both these places, and filled them for a month, until Brother Warne came back, and the other work was put in good hands; then he continued the tour of his great field. I give this to let the reader see that it does not mean luxury and ease and privilege to be a missionary bishop; but it does mean a weight of care and responsibility and toil that few have either the strength or the grace to bear.

Chapter VIII.

THE SECOND YEAR.

OUR second year was full of toil and trial. About the last of April, Dr. and Mrs. Rudisill went for a month's change to the hills. We cared for the *Press* and all the other work while they were away, and they were to relieve us when they returned, and give us a month's change. Mrs. Rudisill never fully recovered from her long siege of fever in Bangalore the previous season, and, humanly speaking, ought to have come home before another hot season set in; but she would not urge it herself, and as she could not be spared without loss to the work, no one felt like urging her return. It was hoped that a change to the hills would help her greatly. Mrs. Isham had suffered more or less from pain in her eyes and the back of her head almost from the first of our experience in India, but we hoped it would pass away as she became acclimated. But the many calls on her strength from the work, the care, and the climate, only aggravated her suffering; and as the heat increased, she grew much worse. From this time on, we had the additional anxiety of her declining health.

We had our arrangements made to leave Madras for Ootacamund, the summer capital of the Madras Presidency, on the 20th of May. This was a very trying day. The thermometer registered 110° in the shade, and the wind from the interior was like the breath of a furnace. About one o'clock, Mrs. Isham was looking through a small opening in the *tatty*, when a sharp pain, piercing from the eye to the back of the head, sickened and prostrated her. There is little doubt that it was a slight sunstroke; and from that time she grew steadily worse. We managed, however, to get to the train and start for the hills. Mrs. Isham said afterward that, as we were leaving Madras that evening, she felt that she should not live to return. By the next day at ten o'clock we reached Metapaliam, where we left the railway to ascend the mountains by *touga*. Metapaliam is one of the hottest places on this earth. It is just at the base of the mountains, where the sun's maximum power is unrelieved by either breeze or moisture. It is a common expression, that it is separated from the burning lake by but a sheet of tissue-paper.

However, we managed to survive; and, with such light baggage as we were permitted to carry, started on the rapid journey of thirty-two miles, and an ascent of over six thousand feet. The *tonga* in which we made this journey is a two-wheeled vehicle, with two seats backed together; or, rather, having a two-faced back between them, the seats being low down between the wheels to prevent upsetting. The driver sat facing front; and wife and I, each holding a child, faced backward. We traveled at a gallop, having relays of horses every mile and a half after the ascent began, and reached our destination in about five hours.

The first three miles lay along the level, in the burning heat of the plains, and amid the most luxuriant tropical forest. Here we saw the American conception of a jungle. The plain near the base of the mountains is well watered by mountain rills and frequent rains; and, as the heat is extreme, vegetation is rank and varied. It is only at the base of mountains that the jungle is a dense forest. Most of what is called jungle in India is open country, and as barren as a desert most of the year. Oranges, and many varieties of plantains, and numerous other tropical fruits, are abundant all along these lower hillsides, and in all stages of development from the blossom to the ripe fruit. There can be no more magnificent scenery than that along this ascent. The vast, the luxuriant, and the delicately beautiful so combine as to be captivating beyond description. As we ascend, above the belt of tropical fruits the mountain-sides are clothed in the rich green of the tea and coffee plant. Many Englishmen have large plantations for these products; and, higher up, there are large plantations of cinchona-trees.

After the first ten miles are passed, the temperature is so much lower that one is quite comfortable, and begins to feel refreshed, as now and again a cool breeze from the mountains comes down to welcome him. Twenty miles up from the plains, out come the overcoats and wraps; and the rest of the way, one chills and shivers until he reaches his *bungalow* and sits down by a fire. We needed fire all the time we were in the hills, which was during the warmest season of the year.

Ootacamund is an English town of five hundred houses. It is one of the most delightful spots on earth in many ways. The market part of the town is situated in a basin of the hills; and the residences are villas, scattered everywhere on the mountain-sides. The grounds about the homes are spacious; the flower-gardens are rich in a variety of plants and colors; the hillsides are well wooded with the transplanted blue-gum tree from Australia. All about the town and surrounding country are beautiful and well-kept drives; and all that nature and art can do, is done to make it a delightsome retreat. To one side of the town is situated the governor's mansion, in the midst of one of the most superb parks in the world. It is said to contain a specimen of every tree that will live at that altitude; and there are flowers of numberless varieties. Whether the statement concerning the trees be true, we can not know; but it is true that it would be difficult to find a country on the map of the world whose peculiar forest features are not represented. Once or twice a week the governor's band gives an open-air concert in the midst of this garden; and every one who can, turns out to enjoy it. Some may be surprised that such things are to be found in India. But why not? With nature favorable in every way; with starving laborers begging to be employed for a song; and with revenues at their disposal, and the love of beauty in the heart,—why not have parks, and music, and flowers? At any rate, they do have them. There is not a Presidency-town in India, I suppose, that has not its splendid park, or Governor's Gardens, as they are sometimes called; and, in some cases, these contain fine collections of animals. Tuesday of each week is *Shauda*, or market day, at Ootacamund; and it would be hard to find a better market anywhere. It affords the combined products of the tropics and the temperate zone in vegetables and fruits. Better beef and mutton can not be found; and the food manufactures of both Asia and Europe are offered to the purchaser's selection. Taking it altogether, one would about as soon spend his life at Ootacamund as anywhere else on earth, if only he could have his own Government and friends to live with.

We spent a month here, and were much helped—at least, I was. I put in the time climbing the mountains and chopping wood, in order to recuperate bodily energy to resist the enervation of life in the plains. An amusing incident occurred after we returned to Madras, which illustrates how closely the natives follow the pattern set for them in everything they do. I "run down" the shoes I was wearing, climbing the hills; and when a *chuckler* came to take my order for a new pair, he asked me for an old shoe "for size." I was hurried with work, and handed him one of my mountain-climbers without giving the matter any attention. He was longer than usual in returning with the new shoes, and when he came, to my astonishment, they were as badly run down as the old ones. When I objected to them, the poor man complained: "All the same, like master's foot. Very much trouble makin' poor *chuckler*. See, master! so much stretch-work!" and he pointed to the bulged side of the shoe in proof. The joke was worth the price of the shoes, and the poor man could by no means afford to lose perhaps half his entire fortune; so he got his pay in full. A well-known missionary tells of having a pair of pants made, and when the tailor brought them, he found, on trying them on, that they were patched. He asked the tailor to explain, and he said, "All the same, like master's pattern," and showed the patch on the old pair, given him as a pattern, as his justification. They are so in the habit of doing things just as they have been done for all time, absolutely according to pattern, that they never stop to think of the why and wherefore of anything. On returning to Madras we found it was well for us that we had had a month's recreation; for the burden of work and the nerve-strain awaiting us were all we could support as it was.

Shortly after our return, our presiding elder's wife—Mrs. M. M. Rudisill—was taken seriously ill, and her physician gave us little encouragement to hope for her recovery. We all knew so well what she had suffered before, that it was felt by all the missionaries and near friends that she was going home. As the days passed, she grew rapidly worse. All Saturday night and Sunday, the 6th and 7th of July, the missionaries and near friends from our Vepery Church watched with sorrowful anticipation at Waverly, as their home was called. Sabbath evening it became evident the end was near. With songs and prayers and tears the hours passed. There were fifteen Christian friends present in the sick-chamber. The servants, some of whom had been converted in her service, were weeping in the doorway. The light was turned low; all was hushed and still; the breathing became slower and slower; a smile lit up the kindly face, and some one whispered, "She is gone;" and, as if the presence was too sacred for human speech, each one quietly withdrew without breaking the stillness.

Funerals must follow quickly in Madras. So that of our sainted sister, who had done so much of kindness and of cheer for each of us, was arranged for Monday afternoon. My purpose in this whole account is to show how the people of India regard the faithful missionary. At the hour appointed for the funeral service the church was packed, and the yard and street about it were crowded with people. During the services, which were conducted by the missionaries of other denominations, the people wept in sobs and tears. When an opportunity was given to view the remains, the weeping crowd held the casket long after the time for moving to the cemetery; and when they did move, they would not allow the remains to be placed in the hearse; but members of our English Church took up the casket and carried it, the three English Sunday-schools and the members of our Churches following in procession, and singing appropriate hymns. This is so unusual an order, so spontaneous and indirect, that it shows most forcibly how the people for whom she had laid down her life responded in affectionate appreciation.

Mrs. Rudisill was a true missionary, and had no fears to die in India. She used often to say, when urged to seek to come home: "It is as near heaven from India as from America. If the Lord wants me to go home, it will somehow be made clear; if not, I can stay here." She spent her life ministering to others, and seemed to have acquired the power to forget herself even when suffering. Her husband, entirely broken down by his five years' toil in Madras, was compelled to return to America shortly afterward.

During the first five or six weeks after returning from the hills we had fifteen funerals, from a Church of two hundred members. Enteric fever—a malignant type of typhoid—was epidemic, and we could do nothing but minister to the sick and dying. On returning from the funeral of Mrs. Rudisill, having had no sleep for two nights, we were called to the home of an Englishman before we had had time to take a lunch; and while trying to help him to shift, he died in my arms. The family were so helpless I had to take charge of all the funeral arrangements. A day or two later I was at the deathbed of a widow, who lived alone. The natives were all about, ready to carry off anything they could steal. The woman died the eighth day, her temperature reaching one hundred and eight degrees or higher. The corpse turned black from fever-poison in a very few minutes; and yet I was compelled to stay in the room, and make an inventory of her personal effects, and seal them up, taking a receipt from the owner of the house—to secure the heirs, the landlord, and myself from injury, until we turned them over to the police authorities the next day. I was in the room for at least an hour, and suffered in no way from it. I conducted sometimes two funerals a day, and gave all my time to the sick and dying. The people used often to send for me in the middle of the night, and I always went gladly. If the people would treat their pastors so in America, they would get more good from them. It often happens that when sickness is in the family, the pastor would be glad to call; but not knowing it, he fails to do so, and often is met with unkindly complaint afterward. People never complain if the doctor does not call without notice; but they expect the preacher, with perhaps many times the constituency of the doctor, to know all about their ills. It is a good rule to send for the doctor and notify the preacher at the same time.

Chapter IX.

THE ENGLISH WORK.

DURING the two years in Madras, our English work required regularly two sermons each Sunday at Vepery. We had here a congregation in the evening of from two to three hundred, and of about one hundred in the morning. The evening service is the principal one everywhere in India. The Vepery congregation required as good preaching as a good Church does anywhere, to hold the people. Dr. Rudisill, who had been for years a presiding elder in the Baltimore Conference, had been my predecessor for three years; and educated Englishmen, missionaries, and sometimes members of the governor's council, were present. While these persons deserve no better preaching than any others, yet their presence in our churches proves that they enjoy our services better than those of the Established Churches, and mightily confirms our own people in their respect and confidence for their own Church. Besides, these English friends often give us the most substantial financial aid in both our English and native work, and their friendship is in every way helpful. So the standard of excellence in our English Churches in India must be kept high, and the best preachers are needed as much as anywhere. This made my study work very exacting, for I had had but little experience as a pastor before taking this charge. On Monday nights I preached regularly at Otary, a suburban village of railway mechanics. Nearly all the people here belonged to our Church, and owned a very neat chapel, which served as a school-house during the week. Then we had class and prayer and League and other social or literary meetings for almost every night of the week.

The most satisfactory work I did, though, was the pastoral work. The difficulty in this work, everywhere, is in the impossibility of meeting all the members of the family together. In America the men are off to business, office, or work early in the morning, and the children are at school all day. The afternoon is the time set for the pastor to call, and his meeting is with the mother and infant children. He does much good by visiting and praying in the homes even under these limitations, but how much more good he could accomplish if he could occasionally meet the whole family together! In India, the man of the house seldom goes to his office before eight, and usually not before nine or ten o'clock. So I devised the plan of sending a printed notice—with date and time filled in—the day before I called, stating that I should like to meet the entire family for worship. If it was not convenient for them to receive me, they could set another time. I went calling both morning and evening; and many, many were the precious seasons had at the family altars of our Church. In this way the pastor can encourage family worship. I made from three to five visits each morning and evening, and so got through a great deal of this work every month. I never got so near, nor felt that I was in a position to be so practically helpful, to the people of any other Church.

We held several special revival efforts, as our strength would permit. We had some conversions in each. The largest number that professed to accept Christ at any one time, I believe, was eleven. The Eurasians are not moved by these special efforts as we often are, here in America. They are steadier—make more of their religion all the time, and less of spasmodic efforts; so, if other things were equal, a Church would not fluctuate as is so often the case in America. The people are naturally quiet, affectionate, and gentle, and not easily wrought up to the pitch of excitement. Evangelists who have been wonderfully successful in America, are surprised and tried at the seeming utter failure of their methods among this class of people in India. There are lasting results from all genuine efforts, but conditions and natures in America and in India are widely different.

There are many discouragements in this work, as well as in all other religious work. One must carry on evangelistic Church-work in the face of a constant war with ritualism. The Church of England is established, having the power of the Government behind it, and a bigoted clergy paid from the public treasury to man it. If one did not know, he could hardly distinguish these Churches from the Romish; and there is no practical difference to the people, except it be that this English Establishment is directly less oppressive financially, but indirectly more so. There are usually two chaplains to a Church, with a pay of about five thousand dollars a year each. Our Church in Vepery is but one block from a very strong and very "High" Episcopal Church, and lives only by squarely joining the issues and forces of evangelism with those of sacerdotalism and worldly advantage. This is the war our Churches are everywhere waging in India; and the American pastor, when weary and seemingly defeated, is apt to feel discouraged. The ritualistic Church has been long in the field; memories, associations, and family ties bind the people to it; and loyalty to it is often essential to advancement in official and social standing. All these things are against our cause; but still we advance.

Our Church has not been established long enough among the Eurasians for us to bring forth a generation of our own educating. Our members have been won largely from ritualism, and had all their early training there. Though they are as loyal to Methodism as any one can be, yet they are strange to our ways; and many of the less devoted ones show such a lack of moral force! They come to Church with hymn-book and Bible; they bow and say a prayer, on taking their seat; they are reverent for all religious exercises, and would not think of putting the hat on in Church; and one, observing them, would think they are most devout and conscientious,—but they are not nearly so careful about their moral conduct, nor so reverent concerning the temple of the Holy Ghost. And one learns that this seeming piety is the remains of their religious education in "The Church." Mrs. Rudisill remarked to us, when we took charge of the Madras work, as a bit of her experience: "Our only hope of building up a strong Methodism among these people is in the thorough training of the young." This is the wisdom of experience; and every worker in the English field in India comes to realize it. So that now, as many who were formerly children in our Eurasian Sunday-schools are coming to maturity, it is gratifying to find them going forth as missionary assistants and teachers, or engaging in League and other Church-work at home. We are in the beginnings of the harvest from this English work, which is full of promise to the Church in the work of evangelizing India. So while the English work, viewed from the point we view work in America, may seem discouraging, yet from the point of results to India, it is most encouraging.

Besides, these discouragements, there is an annoying show of opposition to the foreign preacher in even the Methodist Eurasian pulpits. But this, one finds on becoming acquainted with the people, consists mostly in talk indulged in by persons having but little influence among their own people, and who imagine they are crowded into obscurity by the usurping and even inferior foreigner. As a rule, the Eurasian Methodists would much rather have an American pastor, and one, too, fresh from America.

It is my experience that the Eurasian Methodists are exceptionally affectionate, appreciative, and kindly attentive to their pastor and his family. One rarely receives the evidences of regard in the service of an American Church that he does from them. They are liberal to a fault in supporting their own Churches, and in giving for missions and all charitable purposes. Though they are much less demonstrative in times of revival, and when deeply moved religiously, than many Americans are, yet one sees clear and beautiful conversions and convincing evidences of the Spirit's work. Summing it all up, I have never spent two such happy years as the two of hard service and seeming sacrifice in the work in Madras; and, if it may ever be, I shall joyfully return to that field. Those days when we were comforting the sorrowing, who hung upon us as their only stay, and cheering the sick, who anxiously longed for our coming, and supporting the dying and bereaved with song and promise and prayer, were so filled with the precious sense of spiritual usefulness that one would gladly fill with them the entire span of his years.

Chapter X.

DIVERSIONS.

I WOULD not have my readers suppose that the missionary life is all toil. Of course there is recreation and diversion. Human nature demands it, must have it, and all parts of the world afford it. Missionary life differs little from any other life, except that it is a larger life—a life of greater sacrifices, and greater services, and greater experiences. It is not without superior diversions. In Madras, perhaps the commonest recreation is an evening visit to the beach. Here is the finest surf in the world. Extending ten miles out to sea from the shore-line is a submerged plain, over which the water is but from ten to twenty feet deep. Then the bottom drops to ocean-depths. When the tide is rising, or when the sea is heavy from storms, the great waves come rolling and thundering and dashing into spray and foam, one behind the other, until sometimes ten plunging surges are chasing each other, to exhaust themselves upon the shore. When the breeze is from the sea, it is cool and refreshing. Along this beach was formerly a waste of sand; but the English have made walks and gravel-drives, and hedges of the casurena-tree—which resembles our cedar, and makes a rapid growth in sand—and made beds of crotons and other flowering-shrubs, so that it is now very much like a park; and a large per cent of English women and children, and many native gentlemen, and a few Englishmen, are at the beach from five to eight o'clock each evening. About once a week, while the governor is in Madras, his band plays; his excellency, attended by his body-guard, drives about, with flourish of trumpets and a great spread; and the bulk of well-to-do English turn out. This, of course, has little attraction for an American after the novelty has worn off; but to ride through the Governor's Gardens, and among the Government buildings, with the surf thundering within hearing, and an Indian moonlight beautifying all, is to feel the peculiar charm which results from the union of the arts of civilization with the indolent magnificence of the tropics. Here is the spreading mango-tree, with its leaves of polished green—the live-oak of India in size and shape; and groves of palm-trees, with their tufts of plumes bending lazily from the top; and a great variety of other trees, of all shapes and sizes, but all alike rich in foliage. And here are crotons, in never-ending variety of shapes and colors; many flowers of beauty,— with a sky of India-blue and a matchless moonlight over all. Unite with this the work of the gardener and the architect—arrange the flowers in beds, the crotons in tasty clumps and rows; clean away all the underbrush and vines from among the trees; set an occasional fountain playing in the moonlight; cross and recross the grounds with well-kept drives; put here a Senate-house, with four immense domes; there, a great palace, formerly the residence of a nabob, but now the Revenue Building; on this other side, the Madras University, with its beautiful surroundings; just behind it, the fine Public Works' Building; and on that other side, the Governor's Palace and Banqueting Hall, with walls so white that they seem built of snow; add to these the music of the bursting waves,—and to ride in a comfortable carriage, driven slowly through it all, affords to one in need of rest a recreative diversion not to be despised. Occasionally—two or three times in a month—we get away from our work, and spend an evening in surroundings such as these.

Then, there are many novel and strange affairs, and celebrations of a religious origin, of a more or less public nature, which are interesting and diverting in the extreme, especially to those who have not been long enough in the country to become accustomed to them. I copy the following from a letter, written to friends at home while we were in Madras, as an instance in point: "Last month we had the Mohammedan fast and feast, called the *Mahorum*; and, as far as I am able to learn, its leading facts are about as follows: It is held every eleventh moon, and lasts ten days. The event celebrated is a quarrel between two brothers—Oosaim and Ahsaim—sons of the prophet. One of them was killed; and the other, escaping, became a homeless wanderer, and was cared for by a tiger. Hence it is sometimes called the 'Tiger Festival.' When this boy grew up, he determined, in memory of all these events, to hold a solemn fast and feast. Originally it was a mourning celebration, on the side of the death of one of the brothers; but on the side of the tiger's hospitality, and the rescue of the other brother, it was a joyous feast; and to this day the orthodox and informed Mohammedans meet and snivel and wail together, with seeming depth of feeling, in honor of this event. There is no meaning in it calculated to produce any lasting effect on character. It is a mere arbitrary observance, completed in ten days, and then dismissed until the time of its observance recurs again."

But this orthodox observance of the *Mahorum*, though the only part having any real significance, is of no interest to speak of, compared with the weird spectacles seen in the streets. The people call it the "Tiger Festival." It is a time when every disorderly element throws off restraint; and during the ten days of the celebration, the city of Madras is an ideal pandemonium. Although the *Mahorum* is of Mohammedan origin and meaning, yet all classes and races of people take part in it. Like everything else in heathenism, it has degenerated into a mere opportunity to exercise the spirit and the enormities of meaningless idolatry. To the reckless it is a time of disorder; to the boorish it affords a chance to appear in grotesque garb, and act the fool; to the designing it gives an opportunity, and to the vicious and bestial it is a time of violence and excess. It is said that no decent native woman is safe on the streets at such a time. Each guild of Mohammedans builds what is called a cage. I know not why they are so named; for the structures resemble miniature mosques. They are similar in shape and material, but different in combinations of color and richness of decoration. They are made entirely by hand—the framework of light sticks, and the covering of many-colored paper and tinsels.

When complete, and brilliantly lighted within, and flashed upon by torchlight without, the best class of these cages are dazzlingly pretty. Each cage is, I judge, twelve feet square, and fourteen feet high—combining the square, the dome, and the minaret of the mosque. During the ten days of the festival, the cages are kept on exhibition in immense booths, and are inspected by multitudes. The finest cage in Madras is that built by the governor's Mohammedan guard; and the crowds visiting its booth are so great at times that many fail to reach the scene.

On the last night of the *Mahorum*, these cages are carried in procession, amid a wilderness of torches, to one of the large pools of the city, dipped in the water, the paper torn off, and the frames preserved for future use; and the *Mahorum* is ended. There is nothing so bad about this part of the performances; but this is only the most nearly decent part.

During the ten days, night and day, the whole city is in disorder. The men of each occupation select a fierce, brutal Mohammedan, put a false scalp on his head, with tiger-like ears, dye his beard, and paint his entire body with spiral stripes of black and yellow, spotting him with other colors. They then drug him with *behug*, the effect of which is to make the man as fierce and bloodthirsty as a tiger. Then they make him the center of an immense mob, keep him restrained, irritate him in every way they can; and, when he is in the rage of an infuriated beast, they open a space before him, let loose a sheep in it, which he clutches, and bites in the neck till he cuts a blood-vessel, and then drinks its blood. There are a dozen or more such processions in Madras every evening of the *Mahorum*. When two of these processions meet, and the tigers come face to face, they fight with all fury; and, unless the police prevent it, the two processions join in a hand-to-hand battle. Were it not for the excellent police regulations, many lives would be lost, and no one would be safe on the streets.

Besides these tiger-processions, with their crowding throngs, many go about promiscuously in hideous false-faces, with blackened bodies shining like polished boots, or painted in all sorts of stripes and colors, and all accompanied by the indescribable din of thumping drums, screeching horns, and weird noises, until one feels he is on a visit to Hades. There are other processions of different or no significance—some, at the head of which gilded hands are carried high on poles (these are called "three-finger gods"); others, with images or banners, followed by noisy throngs, who scatter everywhere a sacred yellow powder. Most of all this is entirely meaningless; and this is the difficulty in describing any of these great spectacular celebrations. There is so much connected with them that has neither historic nor religious meaning! It is done because it gratifies an aimless impulse. And right here is one of the saddest results of heathenism—it renders so much of one's outgoings of soul and energy aimless, meaningless, and waste.

The Hindus imitate whatever they see the Mohammedans do. They paint themselves, paint and drug their children, and drag them half-dead through the streets. Fathers carry naked children, whipping them with stinging switches to keep them screaming in torment; and bands of painted hoodlums meet and fight with clubs. If one native has a grudge against another, he takes advantage of this time to get even with him.

We drove in the thick and center of one of the tiger-processions for some hours one evening, with a party of ladies, in two open carriages. Our horses were often frightened, and many times we seemed in danger; but such was the crowd about us that there was no moving except with it. I am glad we could not get away; for it was an evening long to be remembered. The Mohammedans were very polite to us. They had the whole party completely in their power; but they showed us every kindness, and helped us control the horses when they became unruly.

This is only one of many festivals, all differing in character and significance, which, if one cares to pay attention to them, are full of interest. Then, missionary touring, though hard work, is restful through the changes and camp-life which it affords. And when worn out or much run down in health, a short voyage at sea, a vacation in the hills, or a complete change of station, breaks up the steady drag of life. Besides, there are in all the large cities organizations of all the missionaries, corresponding to the interdenominational ministers' associations here at home. The Madras Missionary Conference numbers one hundred and seventy of the most cultured and experienced missionary superintendents, teachers, and preachers, from all leading Protestant missions. Their monthly meetings are broadening and inspiring. One feels that he is in the councils of the world's best training and thinking when in them. And so the missionary's life is varied. His experience compasses the worst and the best—the greatest trials and sorrows, and the greatest comforts and consolations. God's proportion runs through every life alike; "for as the sufferings of Christ abound in us, so our consolation also aboundeth by Christ." (2 Cor. i, 5.) And a missionary's life differs from another's in being greater in many ways

Chapter XI.

CONQUERED BY BROKEN HEALTH.

FROM the first of this second year the drain of the work and the climate upon our energies was exhausting. As the summer wore on, we realized that it would be impossible for us to live in Madras without relief from the pressure of the burden. After Mrs. Rudisill's death, Mrs. Isham had taken the additional work of editing *Mathar Mithiri*—the *Woman's Friend*—the monthly Tamil zenana paper published for the women who are taught to read by the zenana teachers of the different missions. One can hardly realize the difficulty of this work. It is an effort to bring to the minds of these lifetime prisoners such glimpses from life in the great free world that Jesus gives to woman in Christian lands, that they will catch something of the inspiration and hope which she enjoys. Suppose a child of Christian American parentage were so imprisoned for life that no ray of light from any of our institutions—civil, educational, or religious—could reach her, and she should grow up in utter ignorance of all the world except of two or three fellow-prisoners and of one ignorant man who imposed falsehoods upon her credulity and tightened her bonds of delusion,—how difficult it would be to so present Christian life to her, while still in prison, that it would benefit her in any lasting sense! And yet the task is even more difficult in the case of the zenana woman; for she is the child of a motherhood imprisoned from the centuries beyond the horizon of history. We can not appreciate how utterly undeveloped these women are. They are not women in any other sense than in body and years; otherwise, they are deluded children. It is significant that, when a present is made, these mothers appreciate above everything else the gift of a dressed doll. Only those who have been taught by the missionaries to sew, can make even dolls' clothes; and they, it is said, take as much pleasure as children in playing with dolls. From this, one can see how difficult it must be to find or write stories so suited to their experience, and at once of such a character as to help them to the Christian life. It would be impossible, as a rule, were it not that the work of the editor is supplemented by that of the zenana teacher, who answers the questions awakened by what is read in the paper. There were a thousand copies of *Mathar Mithiri* issued each month while Mrs. Isham was editor. Most of them found their way to the zenanas;

and great good must steadily be accomplished in this way. But with all her other work and care, and the fact that her eyes and head were never free from pain, which was aggravated by the required reading and writing, my wife found this editorial work wholly in excess of her strength. But there seemed no way to escape it. It was Mrs. Rudisill's dying request, and there was no one else who was not as busy, or busier, who could do it. There was, too, a strong fascination about the work that would indispose any missionary to refuse; and so it was undertaken.

Almost continually after our return from the hills in July, Mrs. Isham was in the care of a physician of one sort or another. There are plenty of first-class physicians in most of the large cities and military stations in India. The lives and health of British soldiers and civilians are so valuable to the Government that it pays England to establish and support—at India's expense, of course—an elaborate hospital system. And because this establishment is supported from the revenues of India, and because the Government seeks to do everything practicable to improve the health of the people and the sanitary condition of the cities, by treatment, education, and sanitary regulation, these hospitals and dispensaries are open to all who will take advantage of them. To the poor patient, they furnish free bed, food, nursing, and medical treatment; and those who are able to pay are charged fees rated according to the amount of their respective monthly incomes. These hospitals are well equipped, and manned by the best physicians, graduated from Indian, English, and Scotch medical colleges.

Madras, for instance, has a very large military hospital for men only; another for women only; another for women and children; and another for all classes, called "the Eye Infirmary,"—all supported from the public treasury, and open to patients of all classes and races. Besides these, there are other private and mission hospitals. In connection with each Government hospital, there is an out-patients' dispensary, where all who will may consult a physician, and get his prescriptions filled, without cost if unable to pay. Of course, since the entire system is supported from public funds, it is as much each one's right to partake of its benefits as it is our right to send our children to the public schools here in America. Hence very many of the well-to-do, as well as poor, when sick, seek and obtain admission to the hospitals. During September, Mrs. Isham began an out-patient's course of treatment at the Eye Infirmary. She continued going for weeks, until—after having prescribed glasses, which afforded but slight relief—the oculist said he could give her no further relief, as her general ill-health was the cause of the pain in her eyes. He advised an immediate change of climate.

Our family physician came regularly to our house; and one day told us that his patient was suffering from no organic difficulty he could find, but from a general decline of health—and possibly some mischief was working in the brain—which could be relieved only by returning to America. He felt very sure that she was not going to stand the strain of becoming acclimated to India, and that attempting to remain would very likely cost us her life.

He advised me to write Bishop Thoburn at once; while he would call a physician in consultation, and, after thorough examination, they would, if agreed, certify in writing to her ill-health and need of change home. Our physician had had thirty years' experience in medical service in many parts of India, and he was decided in the opinion that no change of climate in that country could relieve his patient. We wrote to the bishop, and followed it up with the certificate, which the physicians concurred in giving.

We were greatly disappointed and chagrined at the thought of having to give up the battle;

and when Bishop Thoburn's reply reached us, we were sure that he did not intend we should give it up, except as a last resort to save life. He submitted the certificate to a leading physician of Calcutta, who encouraged him to believe that the symptoms it reported indicated a state of health which might be relieved by change of climate in India; and when the bishop proposed to transfer us to Lucknow, we gladly and hopefully consented to it. This set the matter of our change at rest for the time being, and we continued at our post in Madras till after Conference, which met late in January. Bishop and Mrs. Thoburn visited Madras before Conference. Mrs. Thoburn, being herself an M. D., called another eminent missionary physician in consultation, and they encouraged us to hope that we *might* find health for my wife, and continue in the field by changing to the North, though they considered it only a doubtful experiment.

But for myself, this was the most trying time in all my life's experience. It was by no means easy to see clearly the line of highest duty at all times. The conflict in the opinions of eminent physicians, and that between duty to the Church and to one's family; my wife's uncertainty of conviction as to the right course for us to take; the knowledge that every day brought increase of suffering and loss of strength to one so precious to many; the fact that one missionary, whose symptoms had been similar to my wife's, had disregarded nature's warning until she had lost her reason and finally her life; and the ever-increasing pressure of the work as the year drew to a close,—made for us some gloomy months. But I came to see that I was not responsible either for my wife's being in India, or for keeping her there. She would not say, "I must go home;" Bishop Thoburn was not ready to release us, and I could not; so, much as I sympathized with and feared for my wife, I found I still had about nothing to do but to trust in God and obey orders. Bishop Thoburn was tender and sympathetic, but at the same time wisely checked our haste, and conserved both our own and the Church's best interests. He dealt with us as a father, and we shall always feel greatly indebted to him for the kindly wisdom of his counsel and the steadiness of his hand in helping us safely through this time of peril.

I was so connected with important matters in the South India Conference that it was necessary for me to attend it, and our transfer to the North India Conference was not made till the close of our own. The session was held at Hyderabad, the capital of the Deccan State, known as the *Nizam's Dominions*. It was to me a season of great religious refreshing, and of helpfulness on many lines; and I returned to Madras determined at least to be true to God, as far as I could see clearly the line of duty.

I reached home on a Wednesday morning, and found we could sail for Calcutta by Saturday, if we could get packed up and aboard. With much hurry and hard work we were ready by Friday night. Then came the farewell receptions tendered by the League, the Sunday-school, and the Church, on the same evening and at the same place. The Sunday-school gave theirs first. The superintendent presided; and an address, signed by every member of the school, was read, and, together with a purse of money, was handed to us. Then, after a response from the retiring pastor and farewells to the school, the Epworth League, with a different chairman, followed in like order. And last of all came the farewell of the Church. The purses contained about fifty dollars. The artlessness of the expressions of affectionate appreciation proved their genuineness. Major Wm. Marshall, who presided for the Church, broke down in an attempt to express the esteem in which we were held by those whom we had tried to help for two years. His tears and choking emotion were more eloquent than any words could be, and, we felt, truly expressed the sentiments of many hearts. I write this merely to show that these people appreciate the sacrifices and efforts made in their behalf. We were not more loved than any faithful minister and his wife would be—perhaps not so much loved as many are—and yet we have not been shown such affection elsewhere. It was hard for us to sever from a people to whom we were so knit in the bonds of affection, and with most of whom we had walked in the deepest valleys of affliction known to humanity.

On Saturday we were helped and escorted aboard our ship by a large company of friends, very few of whom it is likely we shall ever see again. And so ended our two years in Madras. We had passage on a splendid ship—the *Golconda*—of the British India Steamship Company, and had a quiet, pleasant voyage of four days to Calcutta. Mrs. Isham was so ill that she could not bear the sea-breeze on deck, and so, being confined to her state-room, got but little benefit from the trip.

Bishop and Mrs. Thoburn were away in South India, and had directed us to occupy their rooms, which we were delighted to do during our week's stay in the capital of the empire. We were impressed with the extreme simplicity of the bishop's style of living. The rooms occupied by his family were in the building known as the Deaconess Home. One long room, divided by a curtain partition, served as offices for the bishop and Mrs. Thoburn. This, and a moderate sized sleeping-room, with the regulation bath and dressing rooms, completed the list of their apartments. They took their meals at the Home table, and thus avoided the expense and care of a separate establishment. There was not an article of furniture that could be dispensed with; and while everything was clean and tidy, all was plain and substantial.

Our stay in Calcutta was somewhat restful; but Mrs. Isham had again to submit to the now-become-odious ordeal of medical examination and quizzing, with the usual result of disagreement between the physicians. One advised returning to America; the other believed India had climate that would restore her health. We were treated with great kindness by the missionaries in Calcutta, and would have lengthened our short vacation with them gladly; but our new work—the pastorate of the English Church in Lucknow—had been waiting long for our coming, and we hastened on.

We left Calcutta about eight o'clock in the evening, traveling by rail in a northwesterly direction up the Ganges Valley. Daylight, the following morning, found us in the midst of scenes at once beautiful and strange to us. It was about the middle of February, when the wheat is golden and the poppies in bloom; for these rich wheat-lands are also rich opium-lands. From the poppies grown here the deadly drug, for which England forces China to furnish a market—to the ruin of her people—is manufactured. Fields of gold, of red, and of white interchange; and here and there are companies of harvesters, with hand-sickles, gathering the handfuls into huge bundles for the women to carry to the village threshing-floor. All day we were in scenes like these, broken now and then by villages, towns, and important cities. We passed through Benares—the Mecca of the Hindus—and other places of interest and importance, and reached Lucknow at one o'clock of the second night.

Dr. Mansell—for more than thirty years a missionary in India, and our new presiding elder—met us at the station with a carriage, to take us to the waiting parsonage. We were also met by a delegation of our new parishioners, with a quantity of milk for our children. Such an attention would hardly be expected even in America. But our children were asleep, and this carefulness for them was wholly superfluous. Dr. Mansell's house was in the same compound as the parsonage, and his good wife had a lunch awaiting. We ate, of course; but were too tired and sick to enjoy it at that hour. It was about two o'clock in the morning when we went over to our own home—Dr. Mansell carrying one of our sleeping children, and I the other. Imagine our surprise when we found the great gloomy house stripped of everything but dust. It was just as it had been left weeks before by our predecessor, with dust accumulations added. There were no mattresses on the bedsteads, no curtains between the rooms, no water—no anything, except a letter to Mrs. Isham from a missionary who had recently returned to America, instructing her, in a rather mandatory and warning tone, about her new duties. To make matters worse, the wrong trunks—those of a Mrs. Colonel some one—had been brought from the station instead of our own. Dr. Mansell carried over some mattresses; and we patched up such cover as we could, and lay down—three of us—to sleep, but my poor wife to cry all to herself from nervousness and the sense of insufficiency for the requirements of our new work. If we had been well, this night's experience could easily have been laughed through; but under the circumstances it was rather trying.

To us, this seemed, as we looked at the map, much more of a change than it really was at the time of the year we made it. Lucknow is farther due north from Madras than Milwaukee is from New Orleans. If we had made the change in September, it would have made great difference; and, with the bracing effect of a North India winter, we might have continued to work on there for years. But to reach Lucknow late in the winter, when the sun is returning in power, when all India is dry as a desert, and when the burning winds and dust-storms are setting in, is "jumping from the fat to the fire." North India, from the beginning of March to the middle of June, is hotter, and severer every way as to climate, than is Madras. The temperature rarely goes above 110° in Madras, while it reaches 120° or higher in Lucknow and at other North India points. This is due partly to the fact that the rains on the Madras coast come later by five months than to the rest of India, and partly to the moderating effect of the sea at Madras. Lucknow has continental climate, which, of course, means greater extremes. Madras has continual summer, while Lucknow has a much more decided summer, and a mild winter, with frost and very thin ice.

This change intensely aggravated Mrs. Isham's suffering, and rendered her unable to plan and execute even the household arrangements. We were trying to get hold of our work, and furnish and make presentable our great gloomy parsonage. This was a very trying work, as we had little money and few ornaments. While attempting to get this work done, Mrs. Isham completely broke down. Mrs. Dr. Badley called one day while I was out, and, seeing how utterly hazardous it was to her life to continue to bear any sort of care, induced her to go home with her. The missionaries then took matters into their own hands—sent for Dr. Cleghorn, who, after an examination, advised our immediate return home. Then my wife gave up. She said it seemed the obligation to stay was lifted from her all at once, and she felt it her duty to come. She has never since seen it in any other light. The following quotation, which, without even a thought or a suggestion from us, appeared in the *Indian Witness*—the official organ of the Church in India—sums up, I think, the verdict of the missionaries who were familiar with the facts: "The Rev. Geo. W. Isham and Mrs. Isham had no sooner reached Lucknow than Dr. Cleghorn, so well and favorably known as a medical authority throughout the Northwest, peremptorily ordered Mrs. Isham to America *to stay*, as she is 'constitutionally unfitted for residence in India.' Mr. and Mrs. Isham have done their best to stay. They have remained when others less determined, or less attached to the field, would have given up the battle which Mrs. Isham has waged against pain and weakness and lassitude. They go, regretting their inability to remain, as all the mission staff and their many South-of-India friends regret to spare them. Both have been honored servants of the Master in India. The work they have done will abide."

Chapter XII.

HOMEWARD TRAVELS.

WE telegraphed Dr. Cleghorn's advice to Bishop Thoburn; and, in reply, he directed us to return to America as soon as possible. Our recently unpacked effects were shortly repacked, and shipped to Bombay. Freight travels very slowly in India; and it would take at least a week for our boxes to reach the sea. We concluded to stay in the North until as near sailing-time as possible. We would have at least a week. Mrs. Badley urged me to use the time seeing as much as possible of North India. I visited, however, but two of the great cities; viz., Agra and Cawnpore. The former is the capital of the Province of the same name, which was formerly an important Mohammedan State. An object of great interest here is Fort Akbar, the royal fortress of the Mohammedan era. This contains the celebrated "Pearl Mosque," the king's harem, the palace of Shah Jehan, royal reception-halls, Government buildings, courtly residences, baths, etc.—built mostly of white marble on red-sandstone foundations, ornamented everywhere with mosaics of precious stones and delicate tracery. These buildings are partly in ruins, but largely in a good state of preservation. The British Government has restored in cheaper materials the broken pillars, and parts of the gilded ceilings, so that one can get a fair conception of what they were in the palmy days of Mohammedan glory. This fort is now occupied by a garrison of English soldiers. But the object of greatest interest is the celebrated Taj Mahal, situated in the midst of a forty-acre garden of rich foliage and flowers, about a mile east of the fort, on the banks of the river Jumna. Taj Mahal is a splendid mausoleum, built by Shah Jehan (king of the world) for himself and favorite wife, Noor Mahal, sometimes called Noor Jehan (light of the world). In many respects, the Taj Mahal is one of the most superb edifices in the world. Twenty thousand workmen are said to have been employed for twenty-two years in building it; and its estimated cost is $4,000,000, which expresses but the merest fraction of what its cost would be if erected in this country. The well-kept garden in which it is situated may be entered on either of three sides through a palatial gateway. When I stepped from the carriage at the entrance to one of these gates, I at first mistook it for the Taj itself; but, upon passing through to the veranda on the garden side, in full view of the glorious tomb, as it rises from the rich green of the surrounding foliage under the brilliance of an Indian sun, in the loveliness of its heavenly white, I felt that I was standing in the sacred precincts of the realms of glory. Its proportions, harmony, symmetry, and unity are such that one can hardly think it was made by hands. It is one hundred feet in diameter and two hundred feet in height, built in the form of an irregular octagon, and rising from a marble terrace at least two hundred feet square and fifteen to twenty feet high, which in turn rests upon a red-sandstone terrace of about the same height and at least four hundred feet square. At the corners of the second or marble terrace are lofty minarets; and in the center of the main building rises a magnificent dome, flanked by cupolas of similar form. Both the interior and exterior are decorated with mosaics of precious stones and the most exquisite tracery. The entire Koran is said to be written in the mosaics of precious stones on the interior walls. An echo is produced in the dome, which so magnifies the sound of the voice that conversation is next to impossible beneath it. Common talking tones become like the reverberations of thunder; and a whisper, like the roar of the sea.

The sarcophagi of Jehan and Noor Mahal lie in the crypt below the dome. The reign of Shah Jehan, when this tomb was built, marks the climax of the nation's glory. The kingdom exhausted itself in building the tomb of what they were pleased to call "the king of the world" and "the light of the world." When these were buried, the nation faded away. It is impossible to tell by whom this matchless monument of human genius was designed. It is held by some to have been conceived by an Italian architect who was in the service of the refined and cultured Jehan; but this, on the other hand, is disputed by those who hold to the purely Saracenic origin and character of the Taj. There is no doubt that European architects were employed at the Mohammedan courts. The buildings in the fort at Agra and elsewhere combine European features of all civilized ages with Saracenic principles. But by whomsoever the Taj was designed, it is purely Saracenic in principle and ornamentation. The day I spent at Agra was one full of surprise and pleasure, and will ever be remembered with the keenest interest.

At night, I took the train for Cawnpore, and spent the forenoon of the next day amid the scenes made historic and perpetually of thrilling interest by the heroic sufferings of the English residents during the Sepoy mutiny of 1857. About one o'clock, my family, kindly accompanied by Mrs. Badley, reached Cawnpore; and, taking leave of this good friend and the other missionaries, we started on our long and weary journey homeward.

We reached Bombay on the morning of the second day. The weather was becoming very oppressive, and we were detained here for more than a week, waiting to obtain passage by the best and fastest line of steamers. On Saturday, the 14th of March, we sailed aboard the *Bokhara*, of the Peninsular and Oriental Company's line. We had a quiet passage across the Arabian Sea.

We transhipped at Aden aboard the through-liner *Paramatta*, on her six weeks' voyage from Melbourne to London. Nearly every part of the world was represented on our passenger-rolls. These through-liners are to the seas what through-trains are on land. Feeders from New Zealand, from Japan, China, Malaysia, India, Palestine, Egypt, and adjacent lands, bring mails and passengers to convenient points along the path of the great ships. We spent over two weeks in this sea-home, harmonizing the rest of the world to us, and being harmonized to the rest of the world. The tropical heat continued till we reached the Mediterranean, where we were struck by a cold north wind, which seemed severe to us. Our course was due northwest from Port Said. All the second day we sailed along the coast of southwestern Greece. The atmosphere was so clear that, by the aid of glasses, we could see the shepherds and their flocks on the hillsides, and the people moving about in the villages.

In the afternoon of the next day we landed at Brindisi, Italy. This is the terminus of the Continental Railway, which, excepting the English Channel, connects the Mediterranean with the Atlantic at Queenstown, at the southwest extremity of Ireland, by rail. The mails and hurried travelers take the train—made up at Brindisi of mail-carriages, baggage-vans, and Pullman sleepers—and, hurrying on, reach Queenstown one week in advance of those who come by sea. We lost some passengers and gained some new ones at this landing. We spent some hours in the town; visited the cathedral, and heard the priests chanting their mummeries; saw the benighted women, and an occasional wretched man, worshiping the Virgin's statue; saw others telling their sins, through perforated tin, to a drunken priest, sitting in the confessional box,— and felt these people to be even more blindly pagan, as far as they differ at all, than the Hindus of India. We went through a room where, in large glass cases were kept life-sized images of the Savior as he went through the different scenes and acts of his life, together with images of the leading characters who acted with him. At the time of certain Church festivals these images are carried in procession through the streets. One sickens of everything about him here, and feels, as he sees the crowds of lubberly priests lording it over the oppressed and deluded people, that he would like to hitch them up and make them plow.

We left Brindisi on Saturday evening, and when we awoke the next morning we were in the harbor at Valetta, the capital of Malta. We were here some hours, and, going ashore, had a ramble through the town. Valetta was built mostly by the Knights of St. John, who owned and occupied Malta from the early part of the sixteenth century till it was wrested from them, in 1798, by Napoleon Bonaparte. In 1800 the English wrested it from the French, and it has ever since remained a British possession. The island was originally a barren rock, but has been spread over with a thin soil imported from Sicily, and is now made very productive by careful cultivation. Cotton is the staple product of all the three islands included in speaking of Malta, and much of it is manufactured by English factories on the islands.

Malta grows much delicious fruit—its oranges, olives, and figs being renowned. A clearer atmosphere is not known. Mount Etna, which is one hundred and thirty miles away on the island of Sicily, can be seen at the rising and setting of the sun at all times of the year. There is no end to the objects of interest in and about Valetta. It has one of the finest harbors in the Mediterranean. This, together with its central position and military strength, render the possession of Malta of great importance to Great Britain. It is one of the best fortified points in the world, having vast storehouses for grain excavated in the solid rock. It is the center of the grain-trade between the Mediterranean and Black Seas. It serves as a station for the British Mediterranean fleet. A new Government grading-dock was put in a few years ago, which is capable of receiving the largest war-vessels; and the hydraulic lift-dock is of great benefit to commerce, especially to steamers of the India route, as by means of it vessels can be repaired without discharging their cargoes.

Historically and in architecture Valetta and other points on the islands are very interesting. There are old Roman monuments; Saracenic remains; a chapel, built at the point where St. Paul and the company of his wrecked ship are supposed to have been thrown ashore; the splendid St. John's Cathedral, built by the knights; the armory of this order, containing the finest tapestry, and a very fine collection of knightly armor; the Governor's Palace; the carriage of Napoleon,—together with many Maltese peculiarities and niceties, make one feel that he is at the crossroads of all history and modern civilization. Fortunately for us it was Sunday, and we were thus prevented from buying any of the tempting articles brought aboard the ship or offered on the streets. Maltese lace is celebrated for its beauty, and, being in great demand by travelers, is temptingly displayed everywhere. Bales of it are brought aboard, and the shop-windows are full of it. My wife had a fight for conscience' sake, but refused all offers. She was much comforted when, a day or two afterward, an English manufacturer told us that all the lace we saw in Valetta was made in England, and we could buy plenty of the same patterns in any of the good towns of Britain. It is very difficult, he said, to get real Maltese lace, as it is made by hand by the nuns, and except one could procure it from the priests, he could not get it at all. The English are skillful imitators, and their goods go everywhere. The hawkers from Central Asia will offer fine hand-made camel's-hair shawls to the tourist at way-up prices, and when he presents the rare article to the friend for whom it is intended, he will likely be told that it is an English imitation, made of merino wool, and on sale generally in the home-land. Vast fortunes are made by the sale to Englishmen abroad, at high prices, of ingenious imitations of rare and costly articles.

Sunday noon we swung out again to the sea, and sailed all the afternoon in sight of Mount Etna, crowned with eternal white, but with a vast crater of blackness on the seaward side. For twenty days after leaving Bombay the weather was beautiful, and the sea was often as smooth as glass. It was especially so from Malta to Gibraltar, which we reached Thursday evening. We stopped but a short time, and then passed out into the storms of the Atlantic. Thursday night and Friday were severely stormy, and we were all seasick. Saturday was quieter. Sunday morning was foggy; but about two o'clock in the afternoon the fog lifted, the sun broke through, and the green banks about Plymouth, England, rested our weary, longing eyes.

Our passage was to London, but we could stop at Plymouth. London was yet twenty-four hours distant through the channel, where, it is said, "all the mad winds and waves of heaven and earth meet to fight their battles." So, as we had only light traveling baggage with us, we landed, on a quiet Sunday afternoon, from the harbor whence sailed the *Mayflower* long ago, and for which the first New England settlement was named. And it was Sunday— quiet, English Sunday. The customs officers hurriedly passed our baggage, and we were shortly cozily settled in a snug lodging-house, which had been recommended to us by a passenger from Australia. O, the restfulness, the preciousness, of this quiet Sabbath, after living two and a half years where there is no Sabbath in any true sense! At night I went to the Wesleyan Church. The preacher dispensed the word from an old-fashioned high-box pulpit, but not in such a manner as to make any impression on as weary a listener as I was. There was just one thing that impressed me here and everywhere—it seemed in the very atmosphere—the delicious restfulness. It was Easter Sunday, and Monday was a holiday, and the substantial English farmers came to town. Shops, though, were for the most part closed, and all business suspended. Tuesday we took the train, *via* the seven-mile tunnel under the Severn River, for Liverpool. We were comfortably quartered in the Commercial Hotel by eight o'clock at night. Wednesday morning we secured passage on the *Etruria*, the Cunard liner, to sail Saturday. We spent the rest of the week quietly, as there was little of much interest to us about Liverpool. About noon, Saturday, we went aboard, to finish the voyage.

As our splendid ship started down the river to the sea, I was standing near the foremast. I cast my eyes upward, and found the American flag floating over me. I never before realized how beautiful and precious the old flag is to every true American. We had seen it but two or three times in all our wanderings; and when I saw it floating so proudly from the masthead above me, I involuntarily shouted amid tumultuous emotion, "Glorious flag!" I suspect those Britishers took me for stark mad; but what did I care?—there was the American flag over me. I am not ashamed to glory in it anywhere. We spent the night doubling Southern Ireland, and on Sunday morning were anchored in the harbor at Queenstown. About the time we started from Liverpool, the American mails from Australia, all the Orient, and Continental Europe, were crossing the English Channel from Calais. They were hurried on with the passengers who came by rail, and overtook us at Queenstown. These mails and passengers, together with a great crowd of Irish emigrants, came aboard about noon. It is very interesting to see the excited enthusiasm of these impulsive people. As they drew near enough on the tug to be able to distinguish the ship that was to bring them over, they threw their hats in air, and shouted in the wildest manner. One can imagine something of the emotions which, at such a time, heave in the breasts of these liberty-loving people. Many of them have looked forward for weary years to this time of starting to the land of every good, as they have fondly dreamed. They have toiled for money to pay their passage very much as one would toil to free himself from prison, or to emancipate himself from slavery. There are families here who are going to join husband and father, who has suffered separation, privation, and toil, perhaps for years, that he might better his own and his posterity's condition. There are young women here who go to wed the lovers gone before. And to one who is touched with sympathy for the emotions awakened by human hopes, fears, and struggles, the sight is interesting in the extreme. We often complain of how unworthy the emigrants who come, are of America; but this scene was so touching that I really felt that America was hardly worthy of such enthusiasm; for well I knew that the majority of these people would be sadly disappointed of their hopes. If these emigrants were met as they boarded the ship by a wise, warm-hearted missionary, and religious services were daily conducted among them while on the voyage, much could certainly be done toward the solution of our home missionary problems. While on the voyage, impressions are easily made; and the emigrant is hungry for sympathy, and open to counsel. He has about a week of unemployed time, which, it is likely, he will never have after landing. It is easy to see how much more effectively Christianity will lay hold of these people if it comes with a helping hand when they are in the struggles of their life, and so poor that selfish motives can not be charged, than it can ever do if it is not broached to them till they are settled masters of the situation. I most heartily add my humble second to the motion already made by Dr. Buchtel and other leaders, for a steamship home missionary movement.

We had a somewhat stormy passage across the Atlantic, reaching New York on Sunday, April 20th, having been five weeks and two days on the way from Bombay, and having been traveling and tossing about for three months. How delicious it was to stroll, on that beautiful Sunday afternoon, along the green banks of the gliding Hudson, relieved of the suspense and keen anxiety for the life and health of my heroic wife. But still the thought that we were not permitted to continue in the midst of the Church's glorious conflict at the front, awakened a deeper undercurrent of regret, and, should we allow it, would be a source of continual disappointment and temptation. But regrets save no souls, and help no cause. Since we can not do what we would, we shall try to do what we can, and be contented in the Lord.

Part II.—Missionary Lessons.

Chapter I.

THE WORK AND ITS MAGNITUDE.

CHRISTIANITY is for this world, as well as for the *æons* to come. To interpret its purposes and work, and to confine its benefits in our thought merely to the rescue from this world at death of the few it may convert by direct evangelizing agencies, is to rob it of its grandeur, to render it well-nigh contemptible to the practical mind, and to leave utterly meaningless all the glad messages in God's Word which promise the emancipation of this earth from all its evil conditions.

We hear so often from those who seek an excuse to disobey the positive command of the Savior to evangelize the world, expressions like this: "If the heathen are not enlightened, they will not be responsible; and since God is good, he can not damn the irresponsible; hence, the heathen must be saved, if they are not enlightened; but if they are evangelized, many of them will reject the light and be lost. Therefore, I do not believe in sending them the gospel, and I shall give nothing to help send it." One who so speaks, sees no other meaning or purpose in the Redeemer's work than that of getting souls into heaven. In his own salvation he sees only the hope of getting into heaven. If he does any service, it is to advance his chances of entering the pearly gates. He goes to prayer and class meeting, refrains from worldly indulgences, and gives what little he does to support the gospel, simply to get to heaven. This is selfish Christianity, and is not Christianity at all in any good sense. Jesus never held up such objects before men's eyes to induce them to be good. He set before us that all our seeming sacrifices in following him would enrich us a hundred-fold in this life, and give us life eternal. And Paul says: "Godliness is profitable for all things, having promise for the life which now is, and for that which is to come."

Jesus is making a new earth. The greatest work of Christianity is to Christianize the earth. Making converts is but a small part of this great work. The word *civilize* has crept into our speech, and leads our thinking astray. It is not a distinctively Christian word, and leads us to think there is some great power somewhere—in the spirit of human progress, or in evolutionary laws, or in the discovery of liberty and modern institutions, or in something else apart from Christianity—which is improving the world. But the fact is, this onward and upward movement of Christian humanity, and the betterment of the earthly conditions of the race, is traceable to the power of Christianity. It is true this power is stored in and exercised through various institutions and agencies; but since it comes from Christianity originally, it is more nearly just to speak of the *Christianization* than of the *civilization* of the world.

The difference between the pagan and the Christian worlds is very largely a matter of difference in institutions. In the Christian community we have many institutions which exert a steady and powerful influence for good over every member of society who comes in their reach; while the strongholds of Satan, which enthrall men in the grip of evil, are reduced to the minimum. In the pagan community the reverse of this is true. The institutions are Satanic, and humanity is so held in their grip of evil that it is impossible for men to be or do good. Institutions through which righteousness and light, love and life, are made powerful to bless mankind, are either perverted or eliminated. The State, the family, the Church, the school, are perverted to the enforcement of superstition, oppression, slavery, unspeakable cruelty, and infinite outrage. Christianity is devoted to transform all this, and set captive humanity free, and empower us to reach the circumference of our highest and widest possibilities in the great purposes of our Heavenly Father. To show that human degradation is largely a matter of human helplessness in the thralldom of evil strongholds, think of the results that would follow from transferring five hundred infants from paganism to the life of the children of truly Christian parents here in America; or of changing five hundred American infants of Christian ancestry to the homes, surroundings, and life of children in China, Africa, or India.

But are they responsible for being born in this condition, and must they be lost if we do not get them converted? That is not the point at all. The work of Jesus is to bring about different conditions for unborn generations to come forth into, just as he has already done for a large part of the race. "For this purpose the Son of God was manifested, that he might destroy the works of the devil." The Father hath given to the Son "the uttermost parts of the earth for a possession." And Jesus, through the Holy Spirit, is in the world "to preach good tidings unto the meek, to bind up the broken-hearted, to proclaim liberty to the captives, and the opening of the prison to them that are bound; to proclaim the acceptable year of the Lord, and the day of vengeance of our God; to comfort all that mourn; to appoint unto them that mourn in Zion, to give unto them beauty for ashes, the oil of joy for mourning, the garment of praise for the spirit of heaviness." This is the character of the work our blessed Redeemer is to do now for benighted and suffering humanity everywhere. This is the great work he is doing for us; and this is the work of immediate good he asks us to enlist our prayers, our means, and our very selves with him to accomplish for the race. He leads a spiritual emancipating movement of the John Brown order. Every emancipated soul becomes an enlisted soldier, under command of the Emancipator, to extend the blessed work till all are free.

So much for the character of missionary work. Let this chapter be concluded with a few words concerning the magnitude of the work of Christianizing the pagan world. We hear Christians sometimes complain that we have been giving so much, and for so long a time, that the heathen ought to be pretty well evangelized by this time, and wondering if the time is not soon to come when the missionary expense will cease.

Let us compare a little. India and Malaysia together have three hundred and twenty-five millions of people. The United States has sixty-five millions. In 1890 there were in all India and Malaysia two thousand one hundred and ten Protestant missionaries of all denominations (army chaplains not included). In the United States, in 1886, there were eighty-three thousand eight hundred and fifty-four Protestant ministers. And yet my readers know how imperfectly our own sixty-five millions are evangelized under the favorable circumstances of our Christian civilization. India, too, is the most thoroughly missionaried of any great pagan field on earth, except Japan.

Go a little farther. The Methodist Episcopal Church in, 1891, spent for ministerial support in the United States, in round numbers, ten millions of dollars, and appropriated for all India and Malaysia one hundred and thirty-three thousand dollars. Our Church is the leading missionary Church, and if we have any favored field, it is the one of which I write; so that India is fully as well treated at the hands of our Church as all heathenism is at the hands of all Protestantism. And you will find by a little figuring that, if we were doing as well by India as we are by our own country, we would be doing three hundred and seventy-five times as much as we are. And if Methodism is representative, this is true of the relation of all Protestantism to all unevangelized humanity.

The calculation is simple. There are five times as many people in our Indian field as at home, and we spend seventy-five times as much for ministerial support at home as we do in India; and the product is three hundred and seventy-five. Now, I am not advocating that this ought not to be as it is; I simply use it to show the magnitude of the work of evangelism. With all we are doing at home, how partially the work is done in the midst of our favorable conditions! how vast the work in heathen conditions, where all human forces and agencies are so insignificant in comparison! We are hearing a shout through all the Church over what we call the "great harvest in India;" and yet should this harvest continue at its present rate, it will take two hundred years to bring India to Christ. And it is the most hopeful missionary field on earth, aside from Japan. These facts ought not to discourage any one, in face of our Savior's commission and promise; but they should teach us to strengthen our faith and patience, and inspire us to put forth efforts commensurate with the demands for success in the work. The one great passion of the Christian's life should be, not to see how much he can spend on himself and his loved ones, and how little he can give to bring the race under the power of Christ, but to studiously and prayerfully consecrate himself and his children to Jesus Christ to promote the only truly great work; viz., the world's salvation.

Chapter II.

PERVERSIONS OF PAGANISM.

IF one be ever so doubtful of the existence of a personal Satanic intelligence, he must be convinced of it, if fair-minded, by the subtle cunning, serpentine wisdom, and far-sighted adaptation of pagan systems to withstand the truth, the spirit, and even the blessings of the Christian religion.

I wish in this and following chapters to speak of the perversions of paganism which enable it to resist Christianity and prevent the rapid conversion of the world. I shall speak of those perversions which I observed in India, but which, in different forms perhaps, prevail everywhere in pagan systems.

The first difficulty is the extreme poverty of the people. Not that the country is poor in natural resources. It is by no means one of the richest countries in the world, but it could be made to do much better for the people than it does. In territorial extent, India alone is more than one-half as large as the United States, and by irrigation can be made to produce abundantly in most parts—in many localities, two crops annually. It has some rich gold and silver mines, and many precious stones are too common to have intrinsic value in the markets of the country. India has yielded her wealth to enrich other nations throughout the centuries, while her own people have groveled and suffered in the deepest poverty. It is the effect of paganism to destroy enterprise.

The principle, "Except a corn of wheat fall into the ground and die it abideth alone, but if it die it bringeth forth much fruit," applies to wealth as well as to souls. This great principle the people of India have never learned. Hoarding is the curse of India, and has always been. It collects and holds the treasures of exchange, and thus robs the industries and commerce of sinews and wings, and invites the invasion of civilized and powerful robbers from without. Treasure is hoarded in the form of jewelry. One never sees gold in circulation in India, because the rich natives buy it, and mold it into jewelry, and thus keep their wealth locked up. So everywhere you travel you are in the midst of hidden wealth that you do not dream exists, and oppressed all the time with sights of the abject poverty of the people. I have frequently heard it said that the average income of laboring people in India is about nine dollars a year. Bishop Thoburn makes the liberal estimate of twenty-five dollars a year. This is an average. Many get much less. On this a man supports his family, and often an unemployed relative and his family. The best of them have but one meal and a little lunch a day, and many have but one scant meal a day all through life. There are one hundred millions of people who have no other home or shelter than that afforded by some spreading tree. "The streets and the lanes" of the city, and "the byways and hedges" of the country, afford dwelling-places for one-third the people, as they did at the time our Lord uttered the Parable of the Great Supper. One can call together a congregation of five hundred beggars any day in almost any of the large cities of India, with the promise of a half-cent or some trifling bit of food.

Now, this poverty is a seemingly insurmountable obstacle to gospel progress in India. The one opening which offers young men a chance is the Government service. Appointments to vacancies in Government clerkships are made from among those who make the best record in college. The scramble is intense. Many of these young men were married early, and have families. They work so hard and eat so little that fainting and sickness are not uncommon in the halls of learning, and insanity and death sometimes result.

Mr. Wishard, the Young Men's Christian Association representative from the colleges of America and Europe to the colleges of the Orient, told the writer, in Calcutta, that the deep poverty of the students, their fear of giving offense to natives having influence with Government, and the pre-occupation of their student-struggle after a clerkship that would give bread—or, rather, rice and curry—to their families, made it almost impossible for him to get near them, and made them deaf to the gospel. He said that when he tried to get them to talk of their own religion, they frankly admitted they knew nothing of it, because they have no time to investigate it. Nobody, no mission, no message, is interesting to them, unless it helps them to get food immediately. Starvation has immediate terrors; and one can see from this how the many-sided degradation of poverty shackles human souls, and prevents that freedom of action necessary to accept the gospel offers. The force of this difficulty which the gospel meets, will appear as it is remembered in connection with other hindrances yet to be spoken of.

Paganism perverts—or, rather, destroys—mankind physically. It is said there are no sound bodies among pagans. The poverty of diet, the lack of salt—because of its expensiveness, owing to taxation and Government monopoly—and the filth of person and surroundings, make skin-diseases prevalent; itch, scurvy, rashes, etc., affect all, more or less. The awful diseases of unbridled licentiousness spread and burn among all classes, and poison the whole current of blood and life in their descent to posterity. Scrofula, leprosy, and other dreadful blood-diseases, are quite common. The latter is not contagious, nor is it even infectious, except in the case of persons having moist palms or feet, or except it be contracted through the mucous membrane of the mouth or nose. The pus must have contact with a susceptible skin, and warmth and moisture are said to render the skin susceptible. But it is. hereditary; and in case it does not appear in a leper's children, as it sometimes does not, it is certain to appear in the grandchildren. In pagan lands they neither separate the lepers from the masses nor segregate the sexes. Leprosy could be exterminated entirely if this were universally done.

Besides all these skin and blood diseases, heathen people are the easy victims of all the sicknesses that flesh is heir to. They are utterly ignorant of anatomy and the simplest facts of hygiene. It is commonly accepted in South India, among the ignorant masses, that the stomach is a tortoise, and hunger is his squirming. The natives will sometimes justify the theft of food, on the ground that the tortoise inside compelled them to take it. The heart, to them, is a little whirling wheel; and in the head a bird is supposed to be imprisoned. This is a fair sample of the pagan's science of human anatomy. He is equally ignorant of the relation between health and the environments with which he corresponds. He knows no relation between food and strength, or food and sickness. If he eats half a peck of green mangoes—a luscious India fruit—and then has the cholera-morbus, it does not occur to him that the fruit is the cause of his misery. When he is surrounded by festering filth, whose stench would nauseate a glue-maker, and the cholera breaks out in his home or neighborhood, he does not think to ascribe it to his unsanitary surroundings. He is equally ignorant of the laws of contagion and infection. One sees smallpox victims, when the pock is in full bloom, mingling freely with the crowds in the bazars, and no one seems to avoid them. I have seen children in Sunday-school covered with smallpox scabs. No one thinks of leaving his residence, or taking any sort of sensible precautions, when his home is surrounded by cholera patients. Of course this condition is somewhat modified in the larger cities of India, where thousands of English live, and enforce such sanitary measures as are possible; but of the great masses of raw heathen, the statements do not exaggerate the facts.

Disease to them, along with almost everything else, is sent by the gods. When cholera breaks out in a neighborhood, they put a yellow flag about a foot square over the front door, and daub the front of the house with saffron. This is to charm away the god of the disease. They send for the priest, he being their physician. He daubs the sufferer's body with some filthy stuff—the filthier, the holier—ties a yellow string about his waist, and says some *munthrums* (prayers). That is the treatment for the individual victim. To prevent the rest of the family from taking the disease, he brings a sacred cow, gaudily trapped with decorated leather hangings and bells, with horns painted, and garlands of flowers about the head and neck, and, with smoking censer in hand, drives her through the rooms of the house, all the time muttering prayers to the god or goddess which is supposed to be the author of the affliction. But the filth festers, germs multiply, the disease spreads, and the thousands suffer and die in all their helplessness and night. That there are no healthy heathen is generally true, with exceptions now and then, of course. What a wonderful field awaits the medical missionary!

I come now to the mental perversion of paganism. The thought-systems of pagan peoples are as false as their religion. The devil has sciences in the world. Astrology, alchemy in its modern form, the "black art"—these are Satanic sciences. The pagans are, in all things, "too religious." The fundamental order of things with them is false and illogical, and has been through the thousands of years of their history. Through all the ages they have exercised themselves to believe lies and contradictions, and from his earliest efforts the pagan child is trained to thus pervert his mind. And these perversions are religiously sacred. It is true they are under "strong delusion that they should believe a lie." Such havoc has paganism wrought that it seems impossible for them to think the thoughts of Christianity. It is the common complaint of teachers in schools and colleges that the native mind is almost incapable of logical reasoning. The students are proficient in studies in which the memory is exercised, but very deficient in mathematics and other studies that require analytical thought. The thinking habits of the pagan mind are such as to exclude utterly the right thinking necessary to salvation by faith. Of course this is true in the case of sinners everywhere; but the mental perversion is much deeper and stronger in a pagan sinner than in a Christian sinner. The miracle of conversion must begin farther back, and the transformation is immensely greater. This mental perversion is a barrier in the missionary's way so discouraging that it can be surmounted and overcome only by a faith inspired and sustained by the Holy Spirit.

Their ideas of music are so different from ours that we can not melt them with the power of our songs. They would be amazed at the strangeness of the noise. You will see this better from a little incident that occurred during our first year in Madras. I had opened a large high-caste boys' school, and had a Christian teacher at the head of it. I was very anxious for him to have the children learn to sing. He spoke English quite well, and, after I had repeatedly urged him to have them sing, I asked him one day why he did not obey me. He said, with evident hesitation and embarrassment: "*Sahib*, I can't bray like an Englishman." This was his idea of our singing. It would have about as much of a religious influence over them as the braying of donkeys. They have a musical system of their own, and our Christian hymns set to these lyrics are now being used with great profit in North India. But it was not till within the last two years that the difficult task of reducing their tunes to the musical scale was accomplished; and it was thus made possible for our missionaries to master them. This was done by one of our woman missionaries in North India. But this book can be used only where one of the sixty different languages of India is spoken.

On the line of art in the forms of painting and sculpture, the same depravity of taste is seen. A landscape painting has no meaning to a pagan. His pictures and sculptures are all of idolatry and gross obscenity. He can appreciate no other sort. A lady friend of ours sent us a silken wall-banner, with a picture of the Falls of Minnehaha beautifully painted upon it. An Eurasian woman asked what it represented. When asked what it looked like to her, she answered, "The picture of an organ-stool." This woman was far advanced toward English thought and taste. She was part English stock, was a devout and joyful Christian, lived in English style, and associated with English and Eurasian people. She had always lived in flat Madras, six feet below the sea-level, and had no idea what a waterfall is like, and no artistic imagination to fancy one. This barrenness of mind and heart, and this awful perversion of faculty, seems like a desert waste for gospel seed; but with the showers of grace from the ever-present Holy Spirit, even this seeming barrenness is changed to "good ground."

Chapter III.

PERVERSION OF RELIGIOUS IDEAS.

SATAN'S skill and cunning is nowhere more clearly seen among pagan peoples than in the perversion of what may be called religious ideas.

With them, our religion is sin, and what we call sin is religion. For instance, the newly arrived missionary goes into the bazars to preach in the open air to such a company as can be called together. He goes, conscious that he is of a superior race. He remembers he came from a people of cleanly habits, of decent dress, of physical comfort, of general culture, of free institutions, of the true religion, while the people to whom he has come have none of these things, but the reverse of most of them. He can not help but be conscious of his superiority. The very fact that he is a missionary to them is the assumption that he is on a higher plane, and has come to help them up. But he has also the spirit of humility, and fears that the people to whom he has come will think he thinks he is better than they, and so will not come near enough to him to be helped.

But his thinking is wide of the fact. He has come into an atmosphere of intense spiritual pride. They do not think he is better than they, nor superior. In fact, if a strict Brahman were eating in an inner apartment of his house with the door locked, and it came to his knowledge that the missionary's shadow had fallen across his outside doorstep, he would throw away the remainder of his food lest he should suffer contamination by the out-caste's presence.

The writer was sitting in a compartment of an English railway corriage, with some other missionaries, one day, on our way to Conference. A high-caste native gentleman came in with us, and sat just opposite me. He had some small, round, brass vessels, one upon another, in which he carried different articles of food that had been religiously prepared, and was safely protected from all contamination. With these little vessels he had a few oranges and bananas, which, not being so susceptible of contamination, were carried without cover. I was describing to a brother missionary a variety of orange that he had not seen, and pointed to the caste man's vessels in describing the size. The man threw up his hands, and made a furious demonstration. I had not touched his vessel, and did not understand his excitement; and stupidly picked up one of his oranges as an object of comparison. At this he made a wilder demonstration than before, showed great anger; and on my dropping the orange, jerked it out of the window, parted his little *chatties* (brass vessels), took the one containing water, and poured from it on his hand to wash away the contamination of having touched the same orange I had. I felt in my soul that the man was not complimentary, to say the least. I tell this little incident to show the intense spirit of division and the spiritual pride of the caste people.

One can see from it how an audience in India would receive the primary truths of Christianity—"And hath made of one blood all nations of men;" "We are all created by one God, who is our Father; and we are all equal and brethren in his sight." These statements are in direct contradiction to the primary principles of their religion. With them, men are created in distinct strata; and there can be no crossing the lines by those who were born in one caste into another caste, either above or below him. A man can become an out-caste very easily, but he can not change castes. There is no intermarriage or other social intercourse between the castes. There is commercial intercourse among all castes, and religious intercourse between the Brahman and all other castes; for the Brahman demands contributions, and homage of other sorts, from all other classes. Upon this caste-principle is based the exceptional privileges of the Brahmans—who are deified by it—and the honors and privileges of all other higher classes. Upon the preservation of their caste is based their religious hopes and eternal welfare. So the green missionary, who, in his efforts to make them realize his great love for them, proclaims the Fatherhood of God and the equality and brotherhood of man, will be surprised at the storm of rage he may awaken, if he makes his meaning felt; for with them it is easy to go down, but impossible to go up. The struggle all the time is to retain the level one is born in. So, to them, our great principle of human equality simply brings all classes down to the level of the *pariah* (that is, the soulless out-caste); for it is impossible to bring him up. Now, the Brahmans and other high-castes rule the mob. They play at will upon their superstitions and fears, and can infuriate them even to violence against their best friends and interests.

Take another example. Let the missionary preach, as Jesus did, that "not that which goeth into the mouth defileth a man; but that which cometh out of the mouth, this defileth a man."

His doctrine appears utterly diabolical to them; for they hold as primary that the reverse of this is true. And so intense is their belief in the corruption of unsanctified or religiously contaminated food, that they will die of starvation rather than take the chances of ignorance as to the character of what they eat.

Major Marshall—who has had a lifetime service in the British army in India, and who is a devout member of our English Church in Madras—told the writer, that, in times of famine—which occur about once in seven years, when the thousands are starving in every city—he had tried to give food to starving natives. Seeing a starving man running along the road, falling now and then, and lying till his strength enabled him to get up and go forward, he said he had placed milk and boiled eggs and white bread where this starving man would see it, but would not know who had placed it; then he had withdrawn to where he could see and not be seen, and had watched the famishing man come up, look longingly at the food, and go on to starve without touching it.

And so, in many things, their ideas of sin are reversed. What we believe and do religiously, they avoid as sin; and what we call sin in principle and practice, that they do religiously. Maidens consecrate themselves to lives of shame as a religious service; and many such anomalies occur. So we must begin away back with primary ideas in our religious training; for our terms do not convey to them the meaning we intended.

Chapter IV.

WOMEN IN PAGANISM.

OF woman in paganism it may be said in general that she does much of the heaviest and filthiest work. She builds roads, carries the hod, and does this grade of manual labor generally. The men do the sewing—when any is done—and much of the cleaner and lighter kinds of work. But this is by no means the deepest shadow of the picture of woman's condition. In paganism the beastly, brutal qualities and tendencies of men are developed, and the restraining, refining, and spiritual qualities are suppressed until they seem entirely lacking. Gratitude, mercy, pity, sympathy, and such graces, are strikingly exceptional, while "the works of the flesh" vaunt themselves with fiendish audacity. From this almost any one can see the character and spirit of the average lord of the helpless woman.

But now let us see this helpless woman from her pagan lord's standpoint. She is not a spiritual being—his equal in everything but mere animal force; his superior in many of the finer qualities of spiritual being—as she is in the estimation of every refined Christian man. Quite the contrary, she is an animal creature, who exists for the convenience and service of her lord. A Hindu has a far higher regard for a cow than for a woman. When he is seen upon the streets with his wife—as is sometimes the case among the lower castes—she must keep so far behind him that no one would guess that she is in any way related to him. If you speak to a high-caste man of his wife or wives, he is displeased, if not offended. He has learned that *wife*, in the Western significance, means *partner*, and conveys the idea of equality with the husband. It is humiliating to him. When he speaks of his wife or wives he says, "My female," or "the females of my house." But this is still not the worst phase of the picture.

Did woman occupy merely the position of a domestic animal, she might find some liberty and advantage in the indifference and disregard of the lords of creation. Unlike mere animal creatures, she is the source of calamity and all sorts of misfortune, through her sins, to her lord and other relatives. So she must be imprisoned in the zenana, the house of her husband, from her girlhood to her grave; because, by looking upon other men, and variously in the exercise of her freedom, she may sin, and thus make her very shadow prolific in woes to all upon whom it may fall. It is not, as with us, through the disobedience of a first mother—Eve—and through her tempting of her husband till he shared in her guilt, that all calamity and death have come upon us; but it is through the sins of the wife, or woman now living, that the husband and other relatives must suffer.

Here is the explanation of the cruelties perpetrated upon Hindu widows: The husband was brought to his death by the sins of his wife; her shadow is deadly; henceforth she, if a child, must not play with other children, lest she smite them by her dread spell; her head is shaved; she is limited to one poor meal a day for life; she is avoided by all; she is the victim of every whim, caprice, and brutal passion; and the older she grows, the more desolate and helpless her life becomes. The lowest estimate I have seen of these wretched women in India is twenty thousand child-widows, and nine million widows of all ages. Estimates as high as twenty millions are made. Of course the widowhood is enforced. First, it is a Hindu law that a widow shall not re-marry, for it is the duty of the State to protect the lives of male subjects against these murderous creatures; and, second, no man with any sense about him is going to marry a woman who has brought death to one husband already. Marriage is always a risky business where women have such deadly power; but where a woman has exercised it upon one husband, no other man would wish to be allowed to put himself into such a death-trap.

Now think of the effect of this principle as an obstacle to gospel work. It robs woman of all moral courage—just the thing indispensable to her if she would listen to and obey the gospel in braving all tradition, institutions, priestly warnings, superstitions, and objections of relatives, in fleeing from the kingdom of darkness to that of light. From her earliest perceptions she has been taught that upon her conduct depends the welfare—yes, the very life—of all her relatives, especially of her husband and of those nearest to her. So thoroughly are girls schooled in such teaching that they fear even their own thoughts, they hide their faces and slink away into their dark prison-rooms, and spend their lives the victims of every imaginable terror. O Christians! what chains of hell are these! We Christians know that no people can be converted unless the women are. A people never rises above the moral and spiritual plane of its womanhood. Women in paganism are in the most unevangelizable position possible.

The sphere of Christian woman in saving the nations is as important as that of the brethren. Men have always thought they were sufficient to the task of the world's evangelization, but they are not; for they can not evangelize pagan women. They may get companies of men together, and preach Christ to them with all force and earnestness; but few men will be saved while Satan rules the wives and the homes through the abominations of paganism. The Lord's servants and handmaidens are indispensable to each other in the work of pulling down the strongholds of evil, and building up the Christian institutions—the family, the home, the Church, the school, the State, and the social circle. Just in proportion as woman is important in every line of human life and destiny, it is important that she should be taught what her husband and brothers are taught. This work men can not do, but women can. They are doing it, by finding their way to pagan woman in her prison-home, and there teaching her, with infinite patience and persistence, the folly of her own thinking, and the glad message of life and deliverance in Christ. Woman's work must have all the departments that of men requires, and some special branches— school and zenana work, literature, orphanages, Bible-reading, and all the lines required to make redeemed woman the partner and helpmeet of redeemed man.

How slowly this work must progress; and yet how surely! The gospel has found its way to these depths. It is preached to those in chains. Those sitting in darkness see its great light slowly dawning within and around them. Christian ministers to body, mind, and spirit are doing their patient, hopeful work. Christian civilization, with its inventions, institutions, and its spirit of progressive enterprise, is battering at the walls of the city of conservatism, whose citadel is the tomb of departed centuries. The right of a benighted past to rule the earth in the enlightened present is challenged, the battle joined, and victory has cast the balance with the armies of the new heavens and the new earth.

Chapter V.

THE CONSERVATISM OF PAGANISM.

ONE of the glorious watchwords of Christianity is "progress." Everything must progress or die. The very dead earth beneath our feet is being wrought upon by the forces of evolution; and from out of present cosmos is to come the ultimate "new heaven and new earth."

With us evolution is a universal law, bringing transformation to all the works of God, and man as well. With this idea of progress we associate the idea of improvement. Our progress must be in improvement, to be progress. Our homes, institutions, methods in everything, and our very selves, must be better to-day than we were yesterday; must be better to-morrow than we are to-day. We Methodists, who believe in Christian perfection immediately attained, still believe in progress on all lines of Christian character; but we believe in progress in perfection to perfection.

The first perfection is what God wants us to be and do to-day; the second is that better being and doing of to-morrow. And so we have a progressive standard of perfection, which we hold Christians should continually and progressively attain—always forgetting the things behind, always pressing to the mark.

Christians who differ from us have a fixed standard of perfection which is to be attained in death, according to Augustinian theology; or through the purging of purgatorial fires, according to the Romish doctrine.

But all Christians honor and look to the future. We are to be better in the future ourselves, and men and things of the future are to be superior to the present. Perfection is in the future, and yet to be attained. We orate about "The Coming Man," "The New South," "The World of the Twentieth Century," "The Day of our Lord," "The Coming Resurrection," "The New Heavens," "The New Earth;" and, if we be true Christians, our hearts are full of rich anticipations of joys and glories yet to be experienced. Our "path is as the shining light, that shineth more and more unto the perfect day."

And it is no disrespect to our ancestors for us to do better than they did, but to their honor; for did they not instruct and inspire us?

The dying Methodist preacher voiced the sentiment of departing Christian generations when to his preacher son he said as a last message: "My son, I have done what I could; I pray that you may do better than your father."

But in paganism all this is reversed. The heathen gaze is to the past. Never having heard of redemption and "the glory to be revealed," he still mourns the departure of the perfection to which the Ancients had attained. These Ancients lived among the shadows of the past, beyond the horizon of history. Who they were, no one pretends to know. But they were all-wise and perfect; and what they said and did, and all in institution, method, implement, and writing, is perfect, sacred, holy; and it is the grossest sin to change. The pagan believes that what he has, originated with the Ancients of his race. He accounts for differences by believing that what other peoples have, is best for them, and was given them by the Ancients of their race; but what he has, is sacredly for him. His highest maxim is, "God forbid that I should depart from the wisdom of the Ancients." Hence, he excuses himself from being missionaried in any sense, and from trying to improve any one else.

Things as they are, are as well as they can be. With him, perfection on all lines has been attained in the lustrous ages of the curtained past. The very best thing he can do, is to imitate and copy as nearly as possible, and preserve and hand down his abominations and everything else to posterity.

Now, one can see how this thinking, like a chain of adamant, holds the heathen world in what it is, and impedes (it can not stop) the progress of the gospel and every civilizing influence. The English Government, desirous of developing the resources of India, offered to furnish modern plows gratis to the natives who would use them. The native plow, which the Ancients gave him thousands of years ago, is an upright stick, sharpened and bent forward a little at the bottom, about four inches in diameter, with a peg in the top and back for a handle to be held in one hand, and a crooked beam fastened in front. To this he hitches bullocks, and with it scratches the earth. When sowing rice, he submerges the little field in water to the depth of three or four inches, and then drags his stick around in it till it is stirred into a batter. But when asked to exchange this plow for the English plow, he answers like this: "The Englishman's plow is a better plow than mine; but the Ancients gave the Englishman his plow, and me my plow; so I shall keep my plow, and the Englishman his plow."

In many parts of Southern India they have a peculiar method of drawing water. An arrangement like the old-fashioned booms of the Eastern States, and about as high as a telegraph pole, is set up; but it lacks the weight of stone at one end which our American arrangements had. Instead of that, a man climbs the pole, and, steadying himself with a bamboo pole, walks forward to sink the bucket, and back on the pole to raise it again. A man stands at the well, and pours the water into the trenches. This is for irrigating the fields adjacent. Morning and evening, this poor creature spends a couple of hours, more or less, walking backward and forward in the burning sun, to water the fields. The English have tried to introduce improved ways of raising the water; but the native holds to the old way with all the tenacity inspired by his superstitious veneration.

The fisherman still puts out to sea on the rude *catamaran*, made of three logs lashed firmly together by sea-grass ropes. This he propels with a paddle, about six feet long; and, without clothing, hat, or shade, spends the hot day in the boiling sun on the sea. About him is every sort of the varied sea-craft of the English, from the spledid royal mail and passenger steamship to the fleet, yet strong, pleasure and fishing sail-boat; and yet it no more dawns on the native fisherman's mind to change and improve his craft than it does upon the bluebird to build an eagle's nest.

Apply this to religion, and imagine the reception the missionary will meet with. He may be listened to with curiosity, and received with every mark of attention and courtesy; but when he seeks to enforce the claims of Christianity on the details of practice, the native will excuse himself by saying: "Jesus Christ had the most beautiful character known to the world. He is morally superior to Krishna, or any other of our gods; but he is the Christian's God. He is for you to obey and worship. The Ancients gave us our religion, our institutions, our laws of marriage, the family, our rites and laws of purity. God forbid that we should depart from their wisdom!"

The wisdom of darkness has done its utmost to forge strongholds from which it is impossible to save men; but the wisdom of God is deeper, his power greater. These walls are crumbling; these strongholds are being pulled down; and the mantle of heathen darkness is being lifted from all the earth.

Chapter VI.

BENEFITS OF BRITISH RULE.

THE rule of Great Britain over India was not established by force of arms. It was brought about by the irresistible logic of conditions, necessities, and events, for which the English were not primarily responsible. Britain's first foothold in India was gained by a profitable commercial establishment, having soldiers enough for protection only. English officers and soldiers came to be employed by the native rulers; and English physicians, politicians, and adventurers gained influence in most of the native courts. So, gradually, the English became prominent military, political, professional, and commercial factors in India; and when rival claimants contended for the sovereignty of a State, as very generally happened, one party was pretty sure to ask for the assistance of the powerful foreigners. This gave the English the opportunity to dictate terms to those who were in such straits as to gladly accept whatever they could have guaranteed to them. Where force was used, it was in the name of some native claimant, who, on being established by the help of the English, surrendered the Government into their hands. Many of these native States became hopelessly indebted to the English for such services, and being unable to meet their accounts, turned over their revenue departments and all to more skillful rulers. These native princes retain their titles and honors, and usually enjoy ample pensions from their English masters. Empire in India seems to have been thrust upon England; and now, finding herself under the burden of this responsibility, she knows not how to lay it down, nor to commit it to other hands. England and India are married, and divorce would be disastrous.

Of course it is not meant that England has not used military power in enforcing her rule over India. She could not rule there were her authority not supported by a large standing army. It is meant, however, that she did not originally gain her dominion by military conquest; but having established her sway in necessitous conditions by the dominating spirit of Englishmen, and by their genius for political organization, her rule will continue until it is superseded by the better order it shall bring forth. There is an eternal fitness in English empire in India. No other nation could do so well for India, nor could India be so useful to any other nation.

It is impossible to estimate or state all the benefits of English rule in India. We can only imagine what would be the state of things if India were left to herself, or were governed by some other nation. We know that English rule brings the Western civilization, with all that belongs to it—both the good and the bad—into conflict for supremacy with the ancient systems and institutions of the East. A representative Englishman is a civilization in himself. He stands everywhere for all that is English. Put him down in what conditions or land you will, and, as far as he has the means and the power, he will express himself in building up about him the institutions that have been wrought into him from his infancy. His dogged tenacity for whatever is English, though somewhat trying to those Americans who think that all good and glory are within our National borders, is, nevertheless, the very soul of Anglo-Saxon domination. By it they slowly, but effectively, overcame their Norman conquerors; by it they remain English in all the world; and by it they are making all the world English. Nothing has ever conquered the Anglo-Saxons but Christianity; and Christianity, with the Anglo-Saxons for its missionaries, will conquer the world, just as surely as the ages come and go.

One of the greatest benefits of English rule

in India is, that it makes room for Englishmen. England is so great that it takes an earth to give her people elbow-room. Think of her crowding millions of strong-bodied and strong-souled men and women; of her accumulated billions of wealth; of the serious, practical, industrious, adventurous spirit of her people; of the great number of her great men in all the lines on which greatness can reveal itself,—and do you wonder that her dominion reaches every quarter of the globe; that Englishmen are braving all dangers, enduring all hardships, in searching out the obscure corners and hidden treasures of the earth, and English enterprise and capital are building railroads and telegraphs, and penetrating the wastes of barbarism with the lines of civilization and salvation? It requires, in round numbers, three hundred thousand registered ships to enable the English to transact their share of the world's ocean commerce. It is a great blessing to the world that there is room for this pent-up life and power and activity to be employed to bless and emancipate mankind. What wars, what excess, what ruin this genius and force would work were there not room for them to be expended as they are! India is by far England's greatest foreign possession. Under her sway more than sixteen thousand miles of railway have been built, thirty million acres of land are irrigated from Government canals, a foreign commerce amounting annually to more than seven hundred and sixty million pounds has been developed, and a Government revenue in excess of three hundred and fifty millions is collected each year. English rule, capital, organization, and leadership make this all possible.

India, under the dominion of her present rulers, gets all her people can be induced to receive of the benefits of English Christian civilization. She is being welded into a great empire. Peace and safety reign throughout her borders. The ravages and outlawry of the Thugs and all such tribes and bands have been entirely suppressed. Property and life are in even greater safety in most parts of India than in America. While there is more petty thieving and sneaking crime, daring robberies and murders are almost unknown.

Sati, the burning alive of the widow on the funeral pile of her husband, the offering of human sacrifices to the Ganges River and under the wheels of the Juggernaut car, and in the worship of the goddess *Kali*, the religion of whose worshipers was to destroy human life, and many other of the most shocking cruelties and grosser superstitions and impositions of paganism, have been suppressed. A splendid educational system has been developed. One boy in five and one girl in fifty now attend school, and thousands in all the great centers of population are taking regular college and professional courses. But of still greater significance is it that throughout the empire the preaching of the gospel or of any other religious doctrine is under the protection of law. Under English rule the most aggressive Protestant Christianity is establishing its institutions of enlightenment, humanity, and evangelism, and sending forth the heralds of Jesus to preach the gospel to the salvation of many, and as a witness to all. This is a consummation we are exhorted in God's Word to pray for, "that the word of the Lord may have free course and be glorified;" and he who can read the signs of the times can see the hand of the Eternal Spirit in all these movements, bringing to pass the prophecies and fulfilling the promises of universal evangelism.

Chapter VII.

HINDRANCES FROM CHRISTIANITY.

IT is often said in Christian lands that infidelity has no missionary agencies nor missionary zeal. This is true in reference to the attitude of infidelity to evangelism and the Christian civilization of the world; but it is not true in reference to the spread of the poison of infidelity itself. Infidelity wages no war against the abominations of heathenism. It has no sympathy for the millions in the thralldom of idolatry. Its war is all against our Divine Savior and his truth.

Infidelity never goes to a heathen country where there are no Christian missionaries. It teaches no heathen to read, builds no schools nor colleges, nor orphanages nor hospitals. But after Christianity, with sacrifice and toil, has brought forth a community of educated pagans, in the hope that the light of Christ may reach them through the doorway of this Christian learning, right in the wake of these years of toil and sacrifice comes the poison-current of infidel literature. We hear a good deal of Voltaire and Paine and Bradlaugh and Ingersoll and Huxley and Tyndall in America, but not nearly so much as in the Christian college and university centers in pagan lands.

Madras, India, is one of the oldest English Presidency capitals of the empire. It is the missionary headquarters and college seat for several of the leading denominations of Europe and America. There are between two thousand and three thousand young men in college in Madras every year. As the years have gone by, these colleges have raised up a large and influential educated community. Faith has been destroyed in the old pagan systems; and this community is in a state of religious chaos. The great hope and effort of the missionaries is, that the Christian faith may follow the Christian learning. But just at this point comes from the home of the missionaries—to these educated heathen it seems right from the bosom of Christianity—great bales of every sort of skeptical and infidel literature, the blasphemous denial and ridicule of Christ and his work for men. And all this is done in the name of liberty, progress, and advanced learning, skilled to deceive these children of darkness, whose eyes are only so much opened that they may see men as trees walking—see everything confusedly—minds in the state of chaos from which alone the brooding Spirit of God can bring the order and power of faith. What is true among the educated Hindus of Madras is true of every missionary center of education in paganism. During our pastorate in India, there was, almost in the shadow of our English Methodist Episcopal Church in Vepery, Madras, a distributing center of infidel tracts and skeptical and heretical books. It was in charge of an English Government officer; and every Sunday morning, while I was preaching in the church, he was distributing, gratis, literary blasphemy to many educated natives.

In Japan, and every hopeful missionary field, the work is greatly hindered by this countercurrent, coming from the very heart of our Christian civilization. Gospel-work is greatly hindered, too, by the crimes perpetrated by Christian nations and individuals against the helpless heathen peoples of the world. The Gentiles have ever been the victims of the avarice and brutal passions of the so-called Christian peoples. The present age is no exception. My space-limit allows me only to mention some of the stupendous outrages perpetrated by Christian Governments, or through the legalized commerce of Christian nations.

In the Ganges Valley, northwest of Calcutta, lies the great wheat-belt of India. Notwithstanding there are millions in India itself whose whole lives are spent in semi-starvation, and hundreds of millions elsewhere who are always in want of food, yet, by the hand of the greatest Christian nation on earth, more than half of that rich wheat-land is planted in poppies to produce opium, for which the Chinese are compelled by military power to furnish a market, and to devote their millions to destruction, both soul and body. This blood-curdling crime is committed by Christian England, simply because there is more immediate revenue to be derived from destroying the Chinese with opium than in raising wheat for the hungry.

The people of India were originally, perhaps, the most temperate people on earth. The Hindu and Mohammedan religions both forbid the use of intoxicants. Among all the vices of these people, they were comparatively free from drunkenness. Temperance does not yield a direct, but it does an indirect revenue. Intemperance yields an immediate revenue, but destroys the very source of future revenue. But immediate revenue must be had; and the people must be taught to drink and become drunken. The sap of the palm-tree is very copious; it is also easily rendered intoxicating. It can be gathered, fermented, and, after all taxes are paid, be sold so cheaply that a man can get drunk twice for one cent. When it is sold so cheaply, of course the revenue is small on a small quantity, and hence the people must be taught to consume large quantities to make it profitable. The method by which the largest revenue could be secured was found to be that of selling the right to open *abkari* and toddy-shops, or drinking-places, in a certain district, for from one to five years, to the highest bidder. The public auctions of these privileges were advertised thoroughly, and so managed as to get the highest possible sum for the Government. Then, these avaricious venders were let loose on the people, practically without restraint, to make them drunkards. There were no restrictions as to age. The drink was distributed gratis at first, until the people began to get a taste for it. The people being limited to one meal a day, of course their systems could not long resist the effects of the intoxicants; and the burning appetite was very soon formed. Then the money that should have gone for food was spent for drink; and there is no doubt that millions have thus been hurried to the grave to make revenue for the Christian Government. It brought more revenue to the Government to destroy the people in drunkenness than could be derived from their productive industries; and so they destroyed them. I am glad to say that this highest-bidder system has been changed in the last four years, and its worst features toned down; but not till after the drinking habit had been thoroughly fixed upon the people.

It was found exceedingly expensive to permit soldiers in the British army in India to be married. To prevent this, camps were established in connection with many regiments of the English army for kidnaped women and girls. To protect the soldiers from contagious diseases, a law was passed by the British Parliament subjecting all public women to inspection by the Government surgeons. This legalized the whole matter, and the vice nourished and the crimes perpetrated under this act are simply horrifying. And when, through the agitation of missionaries and Christian women in England, this hellish law was repealed, many leading officials, and even some bishops of the Church of England, made a great outcry against what they called "goody-goody sentiment." How long will it take missionary sacrifice and fidelity to overcome the influence against evangelism which the history of this crime will exert?

I need not speak of the rum-traffic from Christian America by which the people of Africa are being destroyed. Nor need I refer to the recent commercial circular from the State Department of our Nation to other nations seeking to open markets for American distilled and malt liquors. The heartless and cruel avarice of Christian nations still seeks wealth in taking advantage of the weak and ignorant heathen people, and does not scruple to destroy them and spread ruin and woe among them, any more than when the Spaniards robbed, and murdered, and enslaved the defenseless people of the West Indies in the same pursuit. The difference is in form, and not in fact. The method is not so brutal, but the nations still enrich themselves by sacrificing the rights, happiness, and lives of heathen millions. Christian nations have murdered more heathen than they have converted during the nineteenth century.

Roman Catholicism is a great hindrance to evangelism wherever it exists in mission-fields. Sometimes the priests stir up the heathen, and join with them to exterminate Protestant work and workers. But in every place where Romanism and Protestant missions work together, the former interferes with the latter in two ways: First, it requires no change of heart and life in its converts; it makes no spiritual condition to discipleship. It simply substitutes one form of idolatry for another. It requires of converts that they shall be baptized, worship the image of the blessed Virgin, pay Peter's pence, and obey the priests; and assures salvation as the result.

In villages where the people are very poor, and have no temple or image, they paint one side of a large, rough rock near the village with red, and make it their god. The poor creatures will worship any sort of thing or image. When the bronze statue of Empress Victoria was set up in Madras, the natives were so bent on worshiping it that the police had to interfere to prevent it. The Romish priests take advantage of this bent of the people, and attract them to worship statues of the Virgin. I have seen in Madras a statue of the Virgin standing in an alcove over the entrance to a Romish chapel, and the granite base on which the statue stood was plastered with red paint to attract the worship of the idolaters. Romanism is the worst form of idolatry on earth, because it is mistaken for the true light.

Protestant requirements are much higher and more difficult for an idolater to grasp, because they are spiritual, and he can offer no more than the Romanist; viz., salvation as the reward. Besides, the Romanists often use money to buy up so-called converts, in order to get them under their power. In the second place, evangelism is hindered by Romanism through the dead formality and immorality of Romish Christians. The heathen, like the sinner in America, knows nothing of Christianity except what he sees in the conduct of professed Christians. The presence in many pagan lands of large communities of nominal Christians, who exceed the average pagan in the excess, beastliness, and cruelty of their conduct, neutralizes the sacrifices and toils of many missionaries.

It was this religious deadness and moral depravity of the two or three millions of English and Eurasian professed Christians in India that Bishop Taylor saw was the block in the way of the conversion of the heathen. He at once started on his four years' campaign to evangelize these Christians. The success of his efforts, and of those who succeeded him, has given us live English-speaking Churches all over India, and some of the best missionaries in the world.

Chapter VIII.

THE GOSPEL THE ONLY HOPE.

THE people of India are not an inferior race. They are of the same parentage and stock as the Germanic races, which people most of Europe and North America. The Hindu-Germanic family is of Aryan stock, and is superior to all other branches. "The ancestors of the Hindus, the English, and other Aryan nations," says Max Müller, "had once the same faith, and worshiped for a time the same Supreme Deity, under exactly the same name—a name which meant Heaven Father."

If the Hindu branch, that migrated southward from the central Asian home of the family, had come west, and our ancestors had gone south, and thus the circumstances and conditions met by each branch had been exchanged, our positions would now very likely be reversed; and they would be sending missionaries to enlighten us. The great difference we find between these two branches of the same family speaks forcefully for the Divine power of Christianity, which, a little more than a thousand years ago, rescued the Germanic branch from the depths of the grossest barbarism, and enabled them to bring forth the modern age of progress and Christian civilization. The disputing unbeliever would call attention to difference in climate, and other accidental causes, in accounting for the present superiority of both the man and the civilization of the Western branch. It is, however, a mistaken notion that hot climates are not favorable to the highest art, culture, and civilization. Modern science was born in Arabia, the hottest country in the world. The universities of Bagdad, Alexandria, and of other tropical centers, make most of those of which we are so proud in modern times seem almost trifling. Eighteen years were required to complete the course of study. Science, art, literature, philosophy, and religion were all born, and for the most part matured, in tropical or semi-tropical climates. In our boasted modern civilization of the temperate zone, we are merely learning to make practical use of the splendid achievements of those in torrid climes, who, centuries ago, penetrated to nature's heart, and brought to light her secrets.

The fundamental difference is not of climate, nor of any external condition, but of faith—of religion. True religion is a key-position, on which, if one be right, all other things come into order. Having "first the kingdom of God and his righteousness, all these things shall be added." Just so far as we are nearer right in this than our Hindu brethren, just to that extent we are superior to them on other lines. They are in the fell grip of two strongholds, under which a great brood of evil laws and customs, which oppress certain classes to the seeming advantage of others, are brought forth. Thus the whole system, by which every member of the community is degraded and oppressed, is bound upon them by being intrenched in their selfishness and fears. The two strongholds I refer to—in which the entire Hindu community is helpless—are idolatry and caste. Idolatry holds the people down in every sense. In a village, situated in a malarial district of Southern India, a well-to-do native citizen had a mind to build a second story to his dwelling. He informed his neighbors of his intentions; and, after considering the matter, they interfered to check him, giving as their reason that the *swaney*—that is, the village idol—lived in a one-story house, and no man should rise above his god. And they actually prevented the man, who had the means, from raising himself and family above the poisonous surface atmosphere.

A recognized authority on these subjects says: "Caste is the chief characteristic of Hinduism. Caste and Hinduism must fall together; for whatever may be the evils of the former, the masses believe that it has religious sanction, and must be observed at all cost." The late reformer, Keshub Chunder Sen, said: "Were I engaged in the work of reforming this country, I should not busy myself in lopping off the branches, but I should strike at the fatal root of the tree of corruption; namely, idolatry. Ninety-nine evils out of every hundred in Hindu society are, in my opinion, attributable to idolatry and superstition." By what weapon can this blow to "the fatal root" be struck? Many would respond: "Education and modern civilization will prove effective." But, powerful as these agencies are, we regret to say they are not sufficient to work the necessary transformation. The difficulty is, the Hindus love their idolatry and caste. They defend them in the name of national spirit, and of patriotism, and of respect to ancestry, and so on; and keep them intrenched within the citadel of conservatism. Civilization and education are imported novelties to them, that the masses know little or nothing about. When a college graduate starts to England to complete his education, he is bound under the most solemn vows to remain true to the faith of his fathers; and when he returns, with the highest school-training the world affords, he must make expiation for the necessary transgression of caste while away from his native land. It did seem for a time that education, and other Western influences, would conquer these strongholds of darkness; but of late years a strong reactionary tendency has shown itself, and this very education is being turned to the defense of the ancient thralldom. "A whole literature of ponderous tomes is springing up in Southern India, with no other object than the exaltation of caste."

The following quotations are from leading educators long in the service of the Government universities of India. Principal Wordsworth speaks of the large class of educated natives, whose learning is employed to "vindicate superstition and tyranny." Again, he speaks of a notable advocate of reform as "fighting single-handed." Mr. Sherring goes so far as to say that, with some noble exceptions, those who have had the advantages of education are, "of all classes, the most disappointing. With all their weight of learning, the possession of which enables them to carry university degrees and honors, they are perfectly content to mingle among the most superstitious and ignorant Hindus, to do as they do, to obey their foolish *dictum* as law, and to have no other aim in life than to conform to the most rigid usages of their ancestors."

Mr. Cotton, an unexceptionable witness, speaks in similar strain: "Caste exercises a predominant influence among all classes of the community. Educated Hindus are puzzled to make out what they owe to their society, and why they render to caste their tribute of submission, when there is nothing to compel their obedience. Nevertheless, the institution is as powerful among those who disregard many of its rules as it was with their fathers, who rigidly observed them all. They find it as hard to bear excommunication themselves, and are as disposed to inflict that punishment upon wrongdoers of their community, as were their ancestors in the past. They find it as desirable to cling to their caste-fellows, despite many disagreeable features in their life and character, as their predecessors may have done."

Quotations like these, from candid men of experience in all parts of India, testifying to the failure of purely educational and civilizing influences to break the power of idolatry and caste, could be multiplied indefinitely; but one additional on this line must suffice. Principal Wordsworth, acknowledged to be one of the warmest friends of India, and from his position having the best means of ascertaining the truth, makes the following severe remarks regarding the action of some educated Hindus: "I need hardly say that I consider the existence of the Hindu child-widow one of the darkest blots that ever defaced the civilization of any people, and it is the direct and necessary consequence of the system of infant marriage. Some years ago I should have expected that these sentiments would have found an echo in the bosom of every Hindu who had received an English education, and particularly among those persons who were attempting to appropriate the political methods and ideas of Englishmen. I have no such delusion now. I find some of them employing all the resources of theological sophistry and cant, not simply to palliate, but to vindicate what is plainly one of the most cruel, blighting, and selfish forms of human superstition and tyranny. I find others maneuvering to arrest every sincere effort at reform; sophisticating between right and wrong; defaming the character and motives of reformers; and laboring to establish, by arguments as ridiculous as they are insulting, that English domestic society offers a warning rather than an example to Hindus! I find them vindicating early marriage as the only safeguard against universal sexual license, a confession of moral incompetence which I should have thought that any people with a grain of self-respect would have shrunk from advancing."

There are so-called reformers; but their reforming goes no farther than speech-making. A native newspaper thus compares their public and private life: "A Demosthenes at debating societies, whose words tell as peals of thunder; a Luther in his public protestations against prevailing corruptions; a thorough-going cockney in ideas and tastes,—he is but a timid, crouching Hindu in his home, yielding unquestioning submission to the requisitions of a superstitious family."

Education does not give these people the force to free themselves. There are many who long to see caste abolished, and to be set free from idolatry; but they have not the force to break away themselves, and, braving excommunication, become the leaders of a national reform movement. A prominent official of the empire says in a letter to a friend: "Only a great religious revival can furnish sufficient moral strength to work out the complex social problems which demand our attention." To become, like Luther, the leader of a great religious reform, one must rise from his own cringing servitude to that which he would reform, and live and walk by faith in God. The gospel is the only hope; the sword of the Spirit is the only weapon that can strike the effective blow at "the fatal root." *It* is sufficient. Let evangelism go first; then education and all other benefits of Christianity will follow in richest blessing.

The words of the great Dr. Duff may be appropriately added: "What, then, can exorcise this demon spirit of caste? Nothing—nothing but the mighty power of the Spirit of God, quickening, renewing, and sanctifying the whole Hindu soul. It is grace, and not argument; regeneration of nature, and not any improved policy of government; in a word, the gospel—the everlasting gospel, and that alone, savingly brought home by the energy of Jehovah's Spirit, that can *effectually root out and destroy* the gigantic evil. And it is the same energy, in working through the same gospel of grace and salvation, that can and will root out and destroy the other monster evil under which India still groans—*Idolatry*, with its grim satellite, Superstition. As *caste* and *idolatry* sprang up together from the same rank soil of old nature; growing with each other's growth, and strengthening with each other's strength; luxuriating in mutual embrace and mysterious wedlock for untold ages; flinging abroad their arms, 'branching so broad and long' as to smite the whole land with the blight of their portentous shadow,—both are destined to fall together. The same cause will inevitably prove the ruin of both. The same light of sound knowledge, human and Divine, accompanied by the grace of God's Spirit, will expose the utter folly and irrationality of idolatry and superstition, and, at one and the same time, lay bare the cruelty and injustice of that strange, half-natural, half-artificial caste system, which has done so much to uphold them. Then will the stupendous fabric of idolatry be seen falling down like Dagon before the Ark of the living God; while the anti-social, tyrannous dominion of caste will be resented, abhorred, and trampled under foot with an indignation not lessened by the reflection that, over ages and generations without number, it hath already swayed undisturbed the scepter of a ruthless despotism which ground men down to the condition of irrationals, and strove to keep them there with the rigor of a merciless necessity."

Let Milton's noble prayer conclude the chapter: "Come forth from thy royal chambers, O Prince of all the kings of the earth! Put on the visible robes of thy Imperial Majesty; take up that unlimited scepter which thy Almighty Father hath bequeathed thee; for now the voice of thy bride calls thee, and all creatures sigh to be renewed."

Chapter IX.

RESPONSIBILITY OF STEWARDSHIP.

MONEY is power. The use it is put to determines the kind of power. It is saloon power, tobacco power, political, power, social power, fashion power, commercial power, educational power, gospel power, just so far as it serves in these lines. Money is the means by which one sets in motion agencies to do his will, and through which he exercises the influence of his personality and principles upon the world. The selfish and narrow view of money-getting is to regard a man as engaged in the toil of life merely to make a living or to accumulate lucre to spend on himself and those near him. The soul of such thinking is, that earth affords only a scant sustenance, and each one must grab for himself; and the more he can get, the better living he may enjoy. Such thinking rules men in their struggles to accumulate, in their use of the money they acquire, and in their judgment of the justice or injustice of the laws and circumstances by which some get rich while many make only a living. But there is certainly a more ennobling thought for Christians, both as to our own purpose and in judging our competitors. The more money one can make, the greater influence he can wield. Every Christian is responsible to God for wielding the greatest possible influence; hence, every Christian should make all the money he can, without in any way crippling his godly influence, and use all he makes in promoting the highest interests of his race. This implies a comfortable living for himself and family, the education and equipment for usefulness of his children (which means the support of Church and State and school and like institutions); then, the further enforcement of Christian principles and heralding abroad of the glad message of redemption, as far as his means enable him to do. The philosophy of hoarding for money's sake, is idolatry; that of piling up for children, is pessimism.

The world is dying from lack of the felt power of redeemed personality and principles of divinely imparted righteousness. We need more men who are "rich toward God" in their worldly possessions. There are not too many rich men, but too many poor rich men. How did Jesus become poor for our sakes, that we through his poverty might be rich? He invested all he had, even his life, for us, cast his bread upon the waters, and awaits its return to him. He would say to each of us with means small or great: "If thou wouldst share with me, go thou and do likewise." "Then Jesus called his disciples unto him, and said, I have compassion on the multitude, because they continue with me now three days and have nothing to eat: and I will not send them away fasting, lest they faint in the way. And his disciples say unto him, Whence should we have so much bread in the wilderness, as to fill so great a multitude? . . . And he took the seven loaves and the fishes, and gave thanks, and brake them, and gave to his disciples, and the disciples to the multitude. And they did all eat and were filled: and they took up of the broken meat that was left seven baskets full." (Matt. xv, 32, 33, 36, and 37.)

This assembly in the desert is humanity in miniature as it has been spiritually ever since. We have here, (1) The Savior. (2) Twelve disciples, together constituting the infant Church. (3) A multitude of four thousand men, with women and children, probably aggregating at least ten thousand. (4) Great physical need; three days with little food, so hungered that should they have gone to search for food many would have fainted by the way. (5) A very scant supply; not enough for the Savior and disciples alone. (6) Selfish questionings and fear of the unbelieving disciples, and the compassion of the Savior for the host. (7) Nevertheless, the consecration and delivery of what they had to the Master's hand. (8) The multitude satisfied, and much remaining.

This picture indicates *the present spiritual situation of mankind.* Looking from the human side we see, (1) *The Savior.* (2) *The disciples.* One-fifth of the race, or about five hundred millions, are more or less under the influence of Christianity. One-fifth of these, or perhaps one hundred millions, are quite thoroughly evangelized. A still smaller number than this are devout and intelligent communicants—the true followers of Christ. (3) *The multitude.* At least ten hundred millions, or two thirds of the human race, in entire ignorance of the gospel, and all of the other one-third, save one hundred millions, in great spiritual darkness and need. Fourteen-fifteenths of mankind are in almost as great helplessness as men were nineteen centuries ago when the angels first proclaimed the glad news over the moonlit flanks and folds of Judean hills. A vast multitude is still waiting under the cruel oppression of fear, born of the superstitions of ignorance, for a coming Redeemer. They burn in the fires of their own passions. They are galled to despair in the thralldom of the giant institutions of immemorial antiquity. They are storm-tossed and wrecked in voyages to sacred shrines; robbed, murdered, plague-smitten, buried by the merciless simoon in burning desert sands. They are enduring hardships unheard of, sufferings unspeakable, on weary pilgrimages, and in brutal self-tortures in hopeless searches for the bread of life. (4) *The scant supply*. We are not different from the twelve disciples. We ask: "How can we give the bread of life to so vast a multitude?" They said: "We have but seven loaves and a few little fishes." We say: "We are too poor; we can not provide for our own needs. Whence can so much be accomplished here in this spiritual desert? It can not be done. We must look out for ourselves, lest we scarcely be saved from the wreck and ruin of all humanity. Send the multitude away that they may provide for themselves; do not let them look to us, nor ask us to be burdened with them. We have not enough for ourselves." Under such a spirit, many yield to inaction.

But let us try to see as the Savior sees. (1) He has a different spirit, and sees by faith the inexhaustible resources. He is not anxious for himself or the disciples. *He has compassion on the multitude.* For them he is moved with pity, sympathy, love, helpfulness. He rebukes the disciples' selfishness. He would say: "'Have faith in God.' Trust yourselves to him, forgetting your need. 'Give ye them to eat.'" Our lack is not in poverty of means, but in our faithlessness. Jesus Christ is with us as he was with them in the desert. He has not merely left us the gospel as an instrument by which we alone are to save the world; he still remains in the lead of evangelism, and the same infiniteness is behind the consecrated offerings of the Church for supplying the world's soul needs that was behind the loaves and fishes with which Jesus fed the multitude. (2) He sees a very different use to which our scant means are to be devoted. We look upon the little we have as our only supply, and would hold it for our own exclusive benefit; but the Savior requires that it be consecrated to his will and delivered into his hand, not because he is unconscious or indifferent to his disciples' need, but because he wishes to save the multitude as well, and this consecration of the little we have is necessary to that end. "Fear not, O disciples!" hear him say, "as I fear not for myself. You have me for your Savior. You will never lose me nor come to want. You will never lose me, nor be lost while working with me to save others." You, knowing the Savior, are in eternal safety. The multitude with no

Savior is in midnight despair. Notwithstanding all your need, "give ye them to eat." If we will do *all we can*, the Savior will make abundance, the multitude will be saved, and much will still remain.

It is the law of Christian distribution that we must come to the Master of the feast with emptied baskets. The emptied basket shows faith, obedience, enthusiastic love. It speaks a powerful language and is a successful pleader. It is useless to ask for increased power to do good when we are not using all we have. Much of the praying for missions is useless, for the answer is forestalled. When one with basket, pockets, and arms full of ability to send forth laborers into the great unevangelized fields where the grain droops in waiting for the sickle, prays the Lord to send forth laborers, while he tightens his grasp on what God has given him to send them with, be sure his prayer can not be answered, except by some stroke which would transfer his means to more liberal hands. Such praying is mockery and blasphemy. It accuses God of the stinginess of the miserly suppliant.

The littleness of our means is no valid excuse for not delivering it to the Lord. The one talent must yield its return as well as the five, and the punishment for its non-use and the reward of its use are just as great. Given into the Savior's hand, our offerings, little or great, will be as the planted mustard-seed, the little leaven in the measure of meal, the handful of corn on the mountain, the seven loaves and the few little fishes—yes, the cloud no bigger than a man's hand that God shall multiply into amazing greatness.

Selfishness always seeks the hiding of excuse to escape duty-doing. It tries to take a stand against giving to foreign missions, because it is in favor of the home work. This excuse is not valid: (1) Because home and foreign missions have been mutual stimulants. Much more is done at home than would be if we had no missions abroad. The same spirit that sends gospel help to China and Africa, sends it to the foreign influx, the mining-camps, and the city slums of our own land as well. Missions of all kinds are children of the gospel spirit, and he who favors one must favor all. (2) Because Methodism is the greatest home-mission Church in America, as well as the greatest in the foreign work. We all recognize our own land as the most important mission-field on earth for Americans. With even Bishop Taylor this is a common remark.

Let us see how fully our Church realizes and acts upon this principle. Remember that each

Church is a home-mission station, and we are spending over eight millions a year for regular work in America. But leaving this out of the calculation, let us compare only what may be called missionary grants. We gave for the home work as follows:

From the Missionary Society's funds, in 1891,	$478,562 69
Freedmen's Aid and Southern Education Society,	322,656 00
Church Extension (approximately),	225,000 00
Woman's Home Missionary Society, cash and supplies,	316,222 00
Children's-day collections,	74,577 00
Total,	$1,416,917 69

This omits tract and Bible causes, and all that was given to local educational and other enterprises. We sent abroad, the same year:

Missionary Society funds,	$576,042
Woman's Foreign Missionary Society funds,	263,660
Total,	$839,702

This is all that was sent abroad, with the exception of some small grants from the Sunday-school Union and Tract Societies.

Now, let us make some other comparisons, to show what a home-mission Church Methodism is. We had, in 1890, in all, 23,350 churches. Of these, but 581—about two and a half per cent—are outside of the United States. The total value of our church property was $99,000,000, of which less than $2,000,000—less than two per cent—is outside of the United States. We have, in all, 15,877 traveling preachers; but 182 of these, and 122 missionaries of the Woman's Foreign Missionary Society—a total of 304; less than two per cent in all—are beyond our borders. On the line of education, the value of buildings and grounds is, in the United States, $13,000,000. Value of the same in all other lands is $400,000, or three per cent. This was partly received from foreign sources. Value of endowments and endowment properties, in the United States, over $22,000,000; and less than $400,000—about two per cent—abroad, and this largely received from foreign sources.

The comparison shows that only about one-fiftieth of the Church's strength is expended abroad. No complaint is made. This should be so. But no one has any valid excuse for not giving to the cause of missions on this line. While only two per cent of the Church's strength is abroad, eleven per cent of the increase in membership, in 1890, was in the foreign field—total increase, 100,000; out of the United States, 11,000.

We have been praying the Lord of the harvest to send forth laborers, and the laborers are ready to go. Our Missionary Society could send one hundred missionaries in ninety days, if they had the money. We have prayed God to let us Christianize the heathen, and they are coming faster than we are willing to furnish the means to baptize them and give them pastoral care.

Twenty thousand in India are anxiously waiting for us to send them some one to help them to the Christian life. Money is mighty *now* to help the gospel. In India, thirty-five dollars will build a church that can not be built without the money; thirty dollars will enable a pastor-teacher, who can not otherwise give his time to this work, to labor in the blessed harvest for twelve months; fifteen dollars will send a boy to a Christian boarding-school a year; and thirty dollars will keep a young man in college, fitting himself for the ministry, the year through. We have no adequate conception of the power of our little offerings to do good in these lands. Many a Christian squanders the salary of two pastor-teachers every year for tobacco. God gives him the means to send the gospel and a rudimentary education to two communities of people who are famishing for the light; and he selfishly wastes it, indulging himself in a filthy, injurious habit. O for the day when Christians will cease extravagance and waste, and, living in plain and simple style, will devote their means to the service of the Savior's cause! How can a Christian man smoke a five-cent cigar with comfort of conscience, when, in so doing, he consumes one month's Christian schooling of some poor heathen child? The man who smokes one five-cent cigar a day, robs thirty children of their only hope of rising above the cruel thralldom of their hereditary helplessness. Suppose Jesus were living in your place or mine, what would he do concerning this missionary cause? When one has decided this, he has found the line of his own duty. It is a helpful question to ask in other matters, as well.

Let those to whom much is given, give much; but let him who has little, give all he can. Let each boy and girl, man and woman, have his box, not of precious ointment to pour upon the Savior's head, but of savings for the Lord's treasury to give wings and voice to the gospel message, that the wilderness and the solitary place may be made glad, and the desert to rejoice and blossom as the rose.

It seems fitting that the following words from Bishop Thoburn should conclude this little book. May the spirit that actuates him become the common spirit of Christendom!—

"These are wonderful times. This long-slumbering Eastern world is waking up. The Sun of righteousness is mounting higher in the heavens. The darkness of heathenism is beginning to flee away, and Christians are taking heart as never before. The time has come for our dear friends in America to open wide their eyes and see the wonderful signs of promise which God is displaying before their gaze. Every Christian should thank God that he is permitted to live in such an era in the world's history. Let us all prove worthy of our opportunities, and worthy of the blessed name we bear. Let us act and talk and pray as those who realize that they bear the name of the Savior of men and are to be known by that name forever. If all Christians in all lands could only realize for a few short years their unspeakable privileges and responsibilities, the work of the world's conversion would soon be accomplished."

THE END.

www.ingramcontent.com/pod-product-compliance
Lightning Source LLC
Chambersburg PA
CBHW031819230426
43669CB00009B/1193